I'LL TAKE ROMANCE

Edwin Sánchez

BROADWAY PLAY PUBLISHING INC
New York
www.broadwayplaypublishing.com
info@broadwayplaypublishing.com

I'LL TAKE ROMANCE
© Copyright 2018 Edwin Sánchez

Cover image compliments of Evolution Theatre Company

First edition: April 2018
I S B N: 978-0-88145-751-3

Book design: Marie Donovan
Page make-up: Adobe InDesign
Typeface: Palatino

I'LL TAKE ROMANCE had its world premiere on 17 June 2009, at Van Fleet Theatre in Columbus, Ohio, produced by Evolution Theatre Company (Producers Mark Phillips Schwamberger and Paul Lockwood). The cast and creative contributors were:

ANGEL .... Cole Simon
DEE .... Corbin Jones
SETH CHRISTIE /
   JUSTICE OF THE PEACE ..... Mark Phillips Schwamberger
BREE CHRISTIE .... Johamy Morales
GRETCHEN CHRISTIE .... Kiana Harris
GEORGE LANIER .... Tim Dougherty
CHI CHI LOPEZ .... Raymond Caldwell
SALESPERSON / TOY .... Artie Kaufmann
WAITER / BARTENDER .... Clay Finken
SALESPERSON / REPORTER .... Cornelius Hubbard

Directors .... Mark Phillips Schwamberger &
                                                          Paul Lockwood
Stage manager .... Christine Nickel
Assistant stage manager .... Derrick McPeak
Scenic/lighting designer &
   technical director .... Matt McCarren
Costume designer .... Mary McMullen

NOTE ON MUSIC

For performance of copyrighted songs, arrangements
or recordings referenced in this play, permission
of the copyright owner(s) must be obtained. Other
songs, arrangements or recordings may be substituted
provided permission from the copyright owner(s) of
such songs, arrangements or recordings is obtained
or songs, arrangements or recordings in the public
domain may be substituted.

CHARACTERS & SETTING

DEE
ANGEL
BREE
GRETCHEN
GEORGE
CHI CHI

SETH
FLETCHER *(V/O)*
WAITER
SALESPERSON
REPORTERS
BARTENDER
TOY
PHOTOGRAPHER
JUSTICE OF THE PEACE
GUARD

minimum 8 actors

ACT ONE

(Music: Eydie Gorme singing a few bars of "I'll Take Romance." A spotlight comes up on a scrim on which shots of a romanticized New York in muted colors will appear. They should highlight all the traditional lovers places in the city. The carriage ride in Central Park, the fountain in Lincoln Center, outdoor cafes, etc. The shots should be mixed with shots of high end stores, limos, champagne, etc and a cash register. Mix them up, add to them, play with them. The idea should be that for romance to exist there must be money. As the song comes to its high note finish the spotlight on the scrim should become smaller and smaller until it disappears. from the darkness.)

DEE: I don't want to do this.

ANGEL: Dee, you said you'd listen to me.

DEE: I look stupid.

ANGEL: *(Trying to mollify DEE)* Not to everybody. And a lot of these guys aren't going to be that particular.

DEE: Ears, hello? I have ears I can hear what you're saying.

ANGEL: Think of it like an adventure! We've never done this before.

DEE: With good reason.

ANGEL: Okay, remember the opening of *Gentlemen Prefer Blondes*? I'm Marilyn Monroe.

DEE: So what, does that make me Jane Russell?

ANGEL: …Well, more like Thelma Ritter.

(Music up: a song like Britney Spears' "Gimme More" begins.)

VOICE: Now gentlemen, please welcome to the Man About Town Stage—

DEE: She wasn't even in the movie!

ANGEL: How is that my fault?

VOICE: Angel and…Don!

DEE: Dee! My name is Dee!

(Lights come up to full on ANGEL, impossibly gorgeous and his best friend DEE, who looks like a deer caught in the headlights. They are both wearing spandex shorts. ANGEL takes in the room full of men, closes his eyes, smiles and licks his lips and begins to dance. He is ultra confident in and visibly delighted in his own desireability. Taking everyone in and moving just enough to make sure all eyes are on him. If good dancers are good at sex, ANGEL must be amazing. He notices that DEE is still transfixed on stage next to him.)

ANGEL: *(Hisses)* Dance.

(DEE sucks in his stomach and frenetically begins to dance, as if he's been possesed by a demented aerobics video. ANGEL has to physically slow him down. They continue their conversation from backstage under the music. DEE's smile is frozen in place.)

DEE: Dear Diary, 7:01, I debut as a go go boy, 7:01 and ten seconds, ego declared legally dead.

ANGEL: Now stop that. Isn't this fun? Look Dee, we're go go boys!!

DEE: Yeah how about that.

ANGEL: And you know, I actually think love handles look very nice on you.

DEE: I hate you.

ANGEL: They give you character.

DEE: No, I mean, I really hate you. Why did I let you talk me into this?

ANGEL: Because you always do, silly. And because, we're going to get you a rich boyfriend; even if it kills you.

DEE: And it might. So is it just a bunch of guys in trench coats out there?

ANGEL: You're blocking me.

DEE: Sorry.

ANGEL: *(Scans)* ...Third row from the back, ninth seat in from the left. Has a bulging wallet.

DEE: What?!

ANGEL: His shoulder is up on the right side, means he's sitting on a bulge.

DEE: That could be car keys.

ANGEL: Uh uh. He'd shift more. It's his wallet.

DEE: How do you do that?

(ANGEL blows a kiss to the audience, smiles.)

ANGEL: I'll bet you anything he's coming backstage.

DEE: Okay, just remember, you already have a rich boyfriend—

ANGEL: Well, he's not really a boyfriend.

DEE: Boyfiend then, whatever you want to call it, and who knows, maybe he'll pick me over you.

(ANGEL laughs, DEE doesn't join in the laughter.)

ANGEL: Oh, I'm sorry, you were serious.

(The music changes. ANGEL and DEE head off stage. as the lights dim. The man from the audience is there.)

DEE: Hi, my name is Dee!!! *(To* ANGEL*)* How high was my voice just then? *(To man)* And you would be?

ANGEL: Dee, this is Seth, Fletcher's twin brother.

DEE: *(To* ANGEL*)* Your Fletcher?

SETH: Could we talk somewhere in private.

ANGEL: I don't have any secrets from Dee.

SETH: I do.

DEE: I'll go change. I'll meet you in the lobby.

ANGEL: That wasn't very nice, you chased my friend off.

SETH: So you're Angel. *(He looks at him for a moment, snorts.)*

ANGEL: And you're Seth.

SETH: Could my brother be anymore pathetically predictable?

ANGEL: Why thank you. Oh, and you look just like your picture. The one in Fletcher's den.

SETH: You've been to his house?

ANGEL: Oh, many, many times.

SETH: You do know that my brother's a respectable, married man.

ANGEL: Uh huh, does he?

SETH: He's also straight.

ANGEL: Just like you. How did your mother ever tell you boys apart when you were growing up?

SETH: She couldn't.

ANGEL: Betcha I could. Pretty tie.

SETH: *(Off the tie comment)* What? I want you to leave my brother alone.

ANGEL: You do, huh? Can I try it on?

SETH: *(Regarding the tie.)* No. You can't. *(Regarding his brother)* And yes I do. I want you to stop seeing him.

(ANGEL nods.)

SETH: I honestly don't see what my brother sees in someone like you.

ANGEL: *(Regarding the tie.)* Please. I'd love to feel that on me. All silky and smooth. After all, you want me to do a favor for you—

SETH: It's not a favor.

ANGEL: Or coarse and rough. Then you have to do one for me. Tie please.

(ANGEL smiles. SETH takes off his tie, hands it to ANGEL.)

ANGEL: Oh, I don't know how to knot it. You'll have to do it for me.

(Reluctantly, SETH does. ANGEL stares at him while SETH avoids his gaze.)

SETH: Now if my brother calls you.

ANGEL: I'll hang up.

SETH: Or tries to see you.

ANGEL: I'll be busy.

SETH: Well, then, that's settled.

ANGEL: A tie on bare skin must look odd, huh. I don't like wearing them myself, although I've taken off quite a few. Why was your hand shaking?

SETH: When?

ANGEL: Just now.

SETH: It certainly wasn't. ...So, how much is this going to cost me?

(ANGEL smiles.)

SETH: For you to stop seeing my brother.

ANGEL: I just hate talking about money, don't you? It's uncouth. I've seen your wife in the society pages. She's very pretty. Like Fletcher's wife. Almost identical.

SETH: Let's leave my wife out of this.

ANGEL: Oh we will. Now Seth, let's cut to the chase, you want me.

(ANGEL *holds up a finger to silence* SETH's *protests.*)

ANGEL: You want me because, well besides the obvious, just look at me, am I everything you expected?

SETH: I had no preconceived idea....

ANGEL: and hoped for? Let Angel talk, you want me because your brother wants me. And you're certainly not going to let him have something you don't. Isn't that right, Seth?

(SETH *is silent.*)

ANGEL: Why don't you go buy me something pretty. I mean, if you want to.

(SETH *stares at* ANGEL, *his breathing now audible.*)

ANGEL: Do you want to, Seth? Do you want to see what a boy like I is like when's he's grateful? Dare to eat the peach. Just once. Come back at seven thirty, we can go back to my place.

SETH: I...

ANGEL: Or don't. It's up to you.

SETH: What if my brother were to find out?

ANGEL: (*Smiles*) Oh, Sethy, let's not kid ourselves, you'll be the first one to tell him.

(*Slow smile from* SETH)

(Music: a song like The Weather Girls' "It's Raining Men." Lights out on them. Music fades as a message on an answering machine is heard.)

FLETCHER: *(V/O)* Hello, Angel, are you there? Angel? Are you screening your calls? Angel, honey, this is Fletcher. Please, return my call. My calls. Look, I know you're seeing my brother, oh but I know it's not your fault, he probably tricked you or lied to you or ...why are you doing this to me?! How could you pick my brother over me?! I'm sorry, I'm sorry. Please call me. Please. You have my direct line. Day or night. Just call me.

(Lights up on ANGEL *and* DEE *on bar stools, each with a flute of champagne.* DEE *just having heard the message on* ANGEL's *cell.)*

ANGEL: Isn't that cute?

DEE: Adorable. *(He makes a disapproving face.)*

ANGEL: Don't make that face. Besides, I'm going to see him tonight.

DEE: Good, so you're dumping his brother?

ANGEL: No, why would I do that?

DEE: Angel, you don't get to keep both toys. You need to put one of those bad boys back.

ANGEL: Says who? Really. Says. Who? Tonight Fletcher and his wife are going to this big gala at the Met. She's on the board. She'll be wearing a big ball gown and lots and lots of jewelry, and none of that borrowed stuff either, hers is hers. I figure they'll be getting ready to leave at around eight so I'll call him at the last minute and tell him I want to see him. Right now. He'll hesitate, you know, "Oh Angel, that's great, but- " and I'll cut him off. "Now don't you keep me waiting." And I'll blow him a kiss and hang up. Guess who he'll be with tonight?

DEE: What about his wife?

(ANGEL *toasts* DEE's *glass, who doesn't respond.*)

ANGEL: Oh, I guess she'll be embarrassed, but it's funny, isn't it? Oh, come on, it's funny.

(DEE *looks down.* ANGEL *begins to tickle* DEE *until he laughs.*)

DEE: Okay, it's funny, it's funny. Stop.

ANGEL: Kiss my nose.

(DEE *does,* ANGEL *and* DEE *have made up.*)

ANGEL: …You like this watch? Fletcher gave it to me.

DEE: Yeah, it's—

(ANGEL *takes off his watch.*)

ANGEL: Here. For you.

DEE: No, no, don't do that.

ANGEL: Come on. I like giving you things.

DEE: I don't need another watch.

ANGEL: Presents are never about need. It's how people prove they want you. *(Directly to* DEE) And love you.

DEE: Angel—

ANGEL: Ssshh. It's not my fault they're brothers.

DEE: No, but—

ANGEL: But what? *(He takes* DEE's *hand and puts the watch on his wrist.)* There, now doesn't that look nice?

(ANGEL *smiles,* DEE *swallows, nods, a small smile.*)

ANGEL: You don't smile enough. You've got a nice smile.

(DEE *beams.*)

ANGEL: Even with that little gap in your teeth.

(DEE *takes another sip from his champagne to cover his embarrassment, holds his hand in front of his mouth.)*

DEE: What if one of them really loves you?

ANGEL: *(Shrugs)* Isn't it funny? Me with two men, desperately in love with me and you with none.

DEE: Yeah when you put it like that it's hysterical.

(DEE *looks down.* ANGEL *reaches out and gently touches* DEE's *lips.)*

ANGEL: My poor Dee. You're a hopeless romantic. It would be funny if it weren't so silly. But don't you worry. I'll make sure you don't wind up all alone. We may just have to lower your standards is all. What's your minimum height requirement?

DEE: *(Blurts out)* For your information, I have a boyfriend.

ANGEL: What? No you don't.

DEE: Yes I do!!! I said that out loud, didn't I? Danny. His name is Danny. And he's nuts about me. Nuts I tell you.

ANGEL: Okay, I'll play along, since when?

DEE: *(Into his glass as he drinks)* A year. Since last Thursday.

ANGEL: What?

DEE: A year since last Thursday! He's a pilot, so he's away a lot. That's why you haven't met him.

ANGEL: You're such a liar.

DEE: We met at the Monster on New Year's Eve. We've been a couple ever since. He's a Gemini, from Baton Rouge, one of six children.

ANGEL: You're serious?

DEE: Not such a hopeless romantic now, am I?

ANGEL: So my little Dee really has a boyfriend.

DEE: (*Laughs, uneasy*) Yeah, how about that.

ANGEL: And kept it a secret. From your Angel.

DEE: Well, I thought you might criticize him and that would ruin it for me.

ANGEL: You must really love him.

DEE: (*Nods nervously*) Yes. Champagne all around!

ANGEL: Did you tell him about me?

DEE: What's the right answer to that?

ANGEL: I'll take that as a yes. So, he knew all about me, but I didn't even know he existed.

DEE: Till today.

ANGEL: When do I get to meet him?

DEE: Soon, hopefully. He's always flying those friendly skies. I just hope he doesn't take one look at you and dump me.

ANGEL: Does he own the plane he's flying?

DEE: No.

ANGEL: Then I wouldn't be interested.

(ANGEL *and* DEE *drink.* DEE *thinks he's safe.*)

ANGEL: So, pop quiz, if you had to pick between me and him you would pick me, wouldn't you?

DEE: What?

ANGEL: You know, burning building, last parachute, that kind of thing, you'd pick me, wouldn't you? (*Silence*) If you had to choose between us, who would you pick? Me or him? (*Silence*) We don't lie to each other.

DEE: I didn't lie.

ANGEL: We don't keep anything from each other.

DEE: He's just a guy.

ANGEL: Who you trusted your heart to. Over me.

DEE: Oh, Angel—

ANGEL: Say it. "Angel, I would pick you".

DEE: Angel, …I would pick you.

(ANGEL *and* DEE *clink glasses, initiated by* ANGEL. *As* ANGEL *exits:)*

ANGEL: And I would pick you, too. Always. Love you.

DEE: *(To the now gone* ANGEL.) Love you, too.

(Music up, recording of a song like Annie Lennox singing "Money Can't Buy It." The coffee shop slides out as a bar slides in. BREE *and* GRETCHEN, *the uber fabulous wives of* SETH *and Fletcher, check themselves in their compacts.)*

*(*ANGEL *walks in.* BREE *and* GRETCHEN *close their compacts in unison and pick up their martinis.)*

BREE: So, you're the tramp.

ANGEL: Excuse me?

BREE: You'll pardon me for saying this, but having heard so much about you I pictured you as much younger. Bree Christie, Fletcher's wife. And this is Gretchen.

GRETCHEN: Hiddey ho. Emphasis on the ho.

BREE: Seth's wife.

ANGEL: And Fletcher and Seth would be?

BREE: Underwater for all I care, but no, Fletcher's in jail for having shot Seth.

GRETCHEN: And Seth is in the hospital.

ANGEL: Oh my God!

BREE: "Oh my God". Almost believable.

GRETCHEN: Almost.

BREE: So as you might have deduced, things have changed.

GRETCHEN: Check your program.

ANGEL: All right ladies, and I use the term loosely.

BREE: Oh good, he's not just going to roll over.

GRETCHEN: Although I'm sure he has before.

ANGEL: You each get one more jab and then I go in for the kill.

GRETCHEN: Oooh. *(To* WAITER*)* Waiter deary, double mary.

*(*WAITER *ignores* GRETCHEN, *exits with tray.)*

BREE: Well, let's see, if it's just one jab I should really make it count.

ANGEL: Please do.

BREE: P O A.

GRETCHEN: Power of attorney.

BREE: The three most beautiful words in the English language.

GRETCHEN: Delicious.

BREE: Everything is under our control now.

ANGEL: Good, maybe you can finally buy yourself that orgasm you keep hearing so much about.

BREE: Ouch.

GRETCHEN: Double ouch.

ANGEL: It's over. Is that what you're trying to tell me in your highly soused way?

BREE: Oh dear, if it were only that simple.

GRETCHEN: P O A. P O A.

BREE: Fletcher and Seth.

GRETCHEN: The nearly dearly departed.

BREE: Kept you on a much tighter leash than you thought.

ANGEL: A point. Sometime today.

GRETCHEN: He's in a hurry for bad news. Imagine that. Waiter!

BREE: Everything our husbands, and I use that term loosely, gave you actually still belongs to the corporation that we now control.

GRETCHEN: How long does it take to serve a martini in a gay bar? Oooh, made a riddle.

BREE: Clear enough for you or do I need to draw you a picture?

ANGEL: And you'd have me believe that you would let Fletcher rot in jail?

BREE: Why not, he'll finally have some good gay sex for a change. And Seth will join him once he's out of intensive care.

ANGEL: Well then, I will just make a lovely phone call to the press and make your life a living hell. Oh, and I did mention the lives of your children, too, didn't I?

GRETCHEN: No, I don't believe you did.

BREE: Well, look at you. Pulling out the big guns.

ANGEL: They get bigger.

BREE: Oh, I doubt that. You see, Fletcher and I have no children. And if you cared about anybody but yourself, you'd know that.

GRETCHEN: Here here. Waiter, here.

(WAITER *once again flies by with his tray.*)

GRETCHEN: Damn it, you've got to have a dick to get a drink in this joint!

BREE: And Gretchen here has two lovely children.

GRETCHEN: Ann and Andy.

BREE: You think the press is going to turn on her? For you? It is to guffaw. No. You will be, …oh what's the word I'm looking for?

GRETCHEN: Pariah.

BREE: That's the one.

ANGEL: …Here's the deal. The only deal. I will collect one million dollars from each of you and you will both go on your merry alcoholic way.

GRETCHEN: Did this Mary just call us merry?

BREE: Interesting. Here's the counter offer.

ANGEL: No counter offers will be entertained.

BREE: You get to leave here with the clothes on your back. Lucky you.

GRETCHEN: Oh come on, let's at least take his pants.

BREE: Your credit cards have been canceled, your apartment is back in the corporation's control, and your car, …time?

GRETCHEN: Five thirty five.

BREE: Is gone. That's our counter offer, slut. Oops, Mr Slut.

GRETCHEN: Good girl.

BREE: It really is all about the breeding.

ANGEL: *(Sinking fast)* You both think you're pretty smart, huh.

BREE: I'm not hearing any evidence to the contrary.

ANGEL: But I'm sure you'd rather make this as neat as possible. That I would just disappear.

BREE: Oh, but it's happening right now. You're gone. Disappeared. As if you never even existed. How about that? ...I don't think I ever hated anyone in my entire life. And then there was you.

(WAITER *arrives with drinks.*)

WAITER: Can I get you anything, sir?

BREE: I'll say you can.

GRETCHEN: Whatever you get him, make it a double.

ANGEL: Champagne.

(WAITER *leaves.*)

BREE: I think it's just wonderful we finally had this chance to meet.

ANGEL: Face to lifted face.

GRETCHEN: Look at that. He can still come up with a jab. You've got to love him.

ANGEL: I, ...Can I at least...

BREE: No.

GRETCHEN: But thanks for asking. I can tell my Seth about the pitiful look in your eyes. Sometimes it all just comes together.

(WAITER *arrives with* ANGEL's *drink.*)

BREE: Must dash.

GRETCHEN: *(To* WAITER*)* He's paying.

(ANGEL *nods.*)

GRETCHEN: Oh, one last thing. *(She takes her drink, throws it in* ANGEL's *face.*)

BREE: Gretchen!

GRETCHEN: He didn't even ask how he was.

ANGEL: How...how is Seth?

GRETCHEN: The man who took a bullet for you? How kind of you to ask.

(BREE *and* GRETCHEN *exit.*)

WAITER: Anything else, sir?

(ANGEL *shakes his head "no".)*

ANGEL: Leave the bottle. …And please, don't call me sir. I'm…Angel.

(Time shift. ANGEL *is exactly where we left him, a little worse for wear after a bottle of champagne.* DEE *rushes into bar, coat open, looking for* ANGEL*.)*

DEE: Honey, are you all right? You sounded, I don't know, like…frail on the phone. *(Taking off his coat)* What happened? I went to your place and there were security guards trying on your underwear.

ANGEL: I was sucker punched by two wives with knives.

DEE: What?

ANGEL: The Christie women, they've taken everything.

DEE: My poor baby.

ANGEL: *(Still reeling)* Don't say poor. Everything gone. Everything. Just like that. I don't even have a place to stay.

DEE: You'll stay with me. For as long as you need.

ANGEL: As if I never even existed. How is that even possible? I'm Angel. Do you know how many drinks have been bought here in my honor? Any idea? Ball park figure? Come on.

(DEE *holds* ANGEL*'s hand.)*

DEE: Hundreds.

ANGEL: Try thousands. I couldn't even make eye contact with anybody without people falling in lust with me.

DEE: Maybe you should see this as a wake up call.

ANGEL: Oh I have. Where are you? Stop moving. It's time I realized that if I am the ultimate prize , and I am, I need to find the ultimate winner. The one who really deserves everything that is me. That is Angel.

DEE: You mean someone who truly loves you?

ANGEL: Have we just met? No, him.

(ANGEL *points to an unseen T V monitor over the bar. Lights come up on* GEORGE LANIER *in a tuxedo. A flash bulb goes off, he smiles shyly. Think bashful, awkward, sincere and a head bobber and you have him. Early 50s and a fine specimen of a man.)*

ANGEL: He's been on T V all day. George Lanier. One of the richest men in the world. Maybe the richest. And he just came out of the closet.

DEE: Good for him.

ANGEL: And good for me. He has Angel written all over him. A little rough around the edges but I can smooth him out. *(He blows a kiss towards* GEORGE.*)* Just look at him. If Jimmy Stewart and Gary Cooper had a baby, that's what he'd look like.

DEE: Doesn't have a prayer, does he?

(ANGEL *gets up, his confidence restored.)*

DEE: You'll be back! Bigger and better than ever!

ANGEL: I am big! It's the men that got small. Cold out?

DEE: Freezing. But, we can share my….

(ANGEL *puts on* DEE's *coat.)*

DEE: …or you can wear it.

ANGEL: Mine was in the car. Which they also took. Did I mention I was carless, too?

(ANGEL *leaves.* DEE *pulls up his collar and follows him out. Music: Bizet's* Carmen, La Habanera. GEORGE *is now flanked by* GRETCHEN *and* BREE, *think big dresses, who stand next to him, a giant mockup of a check held between them, large photo op smiles pasted on their faces. They are in an art gallery.)*

GRETCHEN: …and we're excited—

BREE: So excited.

GRETCHEN: …to accept this very generous donation on behalf of, what was it again?

BREE: Something worthy.

GRETCHEN: There you go.

(More flash bulbs go off.)

GEORGE: *(Clears his throat)* It's for an arts program in public schools.

BREE: Yeah, uh huh, actually we're very interested in speaking to you about a new organization.

GRETCHEN: For the wives of corporate heads who are now doing hard time.

BREE: So little is known about them.

GRETCHEN: Us. And the heartache we endure. For example, Bree and myself have chosen to stay married to our bastards

BREE: We're just a couple of old fashioned gals.

GRETCHEN: But we're not above getting the recognition our nobility deserves. Wouldn't you agree our saintliness has somehow gotten lost in all these attention grabbing causes? Of course you do.

BREE: It's obvious he does.

GEORGE: Ladies, to tell you the truth—

GRETCHEN: Truth? Who said anything about the truth?

BREE: *(Looks off stage)* Oops, they're pouring.

GRETCHEN: I'm parched.

BREE: Arid.

(BREE and GRETCHEN exit towards the booze, dragging along a reluctant GEORGE, who keeps bobbing his head, trying to look interested. ANGEL and DEE enter, both in tuxedos. ANGEL strikes a dashing pose, DEE imitates it.)

ANGEL: You may want to suck in that gut.

(DEE does.)

ANGEL: Where is he?

DEE: If you mean the guy surrounded by every young gay guy in the place, he's over there.

(ANGEL zeroes in on GEORGE.)

ANGEL: Well, he's better looking in person, in any case. What's with the head bobbing?

DEE: That could come in handy.

ANGEL: Will you just look at those boys. Could they be anymore obvious? Shameless. Absolutely no finesse. Go get rid of them.

DEE: What?!

(WAITER approaches with a tray of champagne flutes. ANGEL and DEE each take one.)

ANGEL: I'm certainly not going to be one of a crowd. Make them disappear.

DEE: And how, pray tell, am I supposed to do that?

ANGEL: Have I taught you nothing?

(Beat. DEE takes out his cell phone and heads towards the off stage GEORGE.)

DEE: *(Loudly)* Call for David Geffen! Hello! Call for David Geffen.

(GEORGE reenters, glad to be away from the crowd, carrying an untouched flute of champagne. La Habanera *music up. A cat and mouse game begins with* ANGEL *following* GEORGE *but always turning around before he is caught. paintings fly in and out, a visual maze where* GEORGE *now finds himself following* ANGEL, *just as* ANGEL *had planned. He lets himself be stopped by* GEORGE.)

GEORGE: Excuse me—

ANGEL: All right, you caught me. You can stop following me.

GEORGE: I...

ANGEL: Yes you. *(Takes a sip of his champagne)* Terrible, isn't it?

GEORGE: What?

ANGEL: The champagne.

GEORGE: I don't really know. You see, I don't drink—

ANGEL: We'll have to change that, won't we?

(A painting flies in, ANGEL *sees* GRETCHEN *and* BREE *approaching, he grabs* GEORGE *by the arm and leads him behind the huge painting as the wives enter, just missing them. The women have somehow managed to get their diamond bracelets caught and are now, for all purposes, handcuffed to each other. They try to separate without damaging their jewelry.)*

GRETCHEN: Oh Mr Lanier...

BREE: Mr Lanier?

GRETCHEN: Oh, for heaven's sake, you were supposed to watch him. Careful

(GRETCHEN blows air kisses to an off stage guest forcing BREE's hand to also go up.)

BREE: And leave you alone with David Geffen? I don't think so.

(GRETCHEN *elbows* BREE, *motions to an off stage guest. They exit waving and blowing air kisses in the direction of their next victim, exiting while miming a phone and "call me". The painting rises,* ANGEL *is still holding* GEORGE *by the arm.*)

ANGEL: Someone's been working out. *(He lets go of* GEORGE's *arm.)* You owe me. They were about to hit you up for another donation.

GEORGE: It's a very worthy cause.

ANGEL: I'm a worthy cause.

GEORGE: Why do I think you don't need any help at all.

ANGEL: Why Mr Lanier.

GEORGE: George. What's your name?

ANGEL: A couple of things up front, 1: you should know that I'm a lot more work than everyone else in this room, but I'm worth it, and b: I bore very, very easily. Keep that in mind.

(A flustered GEORGE *takes a drink from his champagne, coughs.* ANGEL *smiles at the effect he's had.)*

ANGEL: Thought you didn't drink. Do I make you nervous?

GEORGE: Oddly enough, yes.

ANGEL: That's sweet.

*(*GEORGE *makes an attempt to give* ANGEL *a kiss,* ANGEL *Takes a sip of his champagne, blocking the kiss.)*

GEORGE: I'm kind of new at this.

ANGEL: Then you're very very lucky you met me.

CHI CHI: *(V/O)* There ju are!

(CHI CHI *joins them. 30s, Hispanic, and a walking tribute to the 60s. Long hair, bell bottoms, love beads and a Nehru jacket.* ANGEL *is aghast.* CHI CHI *is a stereotype, but a stereotype with a brain.*)

CHI CHI: Oh my God I was like looking all over the place for ju, sorry I'm late, I thought ju'd be surrounded by all those Chelsea boys just out for jour money, oh jello, who's this?

GEORGE: Chi Chi Lopez, I'd like you to meet…

(DEE *hurries towards* ANGEL.)

DEE: Angel! You won't believe what just walked in. I'm talking a major fashion don't, the one with the little black bar over the eyes, and— (*Notices* CHI CHI, *exactly who he was talking about.*) —oh, …hello.

CHI CHI: Jes, jello to ju to.

ANGEL: George, this is Dee, my very best friend in the whole entire world. And this is Chi Chi. Don't you love it? Chi Chi.

CHI CHI: Or ju can call me Mr Lopez.

GEORGE: Chi Chi here is my best friend. How about that? Now we can all be friends.

ANGEL: Yes, won't that be fun.

(*As* ANGEL *and* CHI CHI *Size each other up* DEE *tries desperately to fill the silence.*)

DEE: Uh, I love your outfit, Chi Chi. I remember I had a navy blue polyester Nehru jacket with big white buttons, dolman sleeves and it was double breasted okay I'll be quiet now.

CHI CHI: Ju know the sixties was the last time anybody had a conscience, people made a difference back then, ju know what I'm saying? I just live for the sixties. And of course the seventies, because we were making so much headway, politically speaking, before AIDS

came. Stonewall was the beginning but it can't be the
end, so I dress to remind myself, and everybody, that
we are powerful as a political people. We are equal to
everyone.

ANGEL: Yeah, okay, God, I hate politics.

DEE: I think Angel means that it just seems that nothing
ever changes.

CHI CHI: Well not for him. But the world doesn't begin
and end with him.

GEORGE: When I met Chi Chi I knew nothing about
what it was like to be gay. He was the first person I
came out to.

CHI CHI: Oh honey, I outted jur ass. My gaydar is a
finely tuned instrument.

ANGEL: Well, I for one, think you're very straight
acting.

CHI CHI: What the hell does that mean? That butch is
better than nelly? Because I'll tell ju, some of our best
warriors, and that's the word I want to use, warriors,
were total flamers.

(GEORGE *puts a comforting hand on* CHI CHI's *forearm.*
GEORGE's *head bobs a little more noticeably.*)

GEORGE: I don't know what I'd do without Chi Chi.
He's my conscience. He was talking, like he's doing
right here, on the elevator, didn't care who else was
there or that he made some people uncomfortable, and
I saw all the clones that work for me trying to ignore
him. But when Chi Chi got off the elevator I found
myself just following him. To the mailroom. I'd never
even been to that part of the building. But I felt safe
with Chi Chi. Isn't that strange? Fifty two years old
and I never felt safe until that moment.

ANGEL: So, still a mail room clerk?

GEORGE: Oh no, Chi Chi's my consultant now.

ANGEL: So you pay him to be your friend? That's nice.

GEORGE: No, he works for his money. Chi Chi won't even let me buy him a present.

ANGEL: *(To* CHI CHI*)* Why not?! Are you insane?! The man has more money than God! He's supposed to pay, he wants to pay! He has a need to pay! That's part of his charm. *(Referring to* GEORGE's *head bobbing)* Honey, you have got to stop that.

CHI CHI: Lemme ask ju something, if George had no money would ju be here?

ANGEL: If George had no money *he* wouldn't be here.

DEE: Boys—

CHI CHI: So ju like him just for his money, huh?

ANGEL: Of course I like him for his money. It's who he is. Just like he likes me for what I am.

CHI CHI: And what's that, I'm afraid to ask.

*(*ANGEL *stops, smiles, turns to* GEORGE.*)*

ANGEL: Why don't you tell him?

GEORGE: Well, I've never really met anybody like you before.

CHI CHI: Not since Disney took over Times Square.

DEE: Now you wait a second, Angel is the best thing that could ever happen to George, that could happen to anybody. He is kind, loyal and loving and probably the most beautiful person God has put on earth. People just think that he's all surface veneer but there's a real, vulnerable person inside him.

CHI CHI: Way inside.

DEE: He's been my best friend since third grade and I won't have you or anybody else disrespect him.

And we can take this outside even though you could probably beat me to a pulp and I hit like a girl. *(Silence)* Did I happen to mention my nehru jacket?

CHI CHI: Well, honey, ju don't say much, but when ju do, watch out.

DEE: This is why I don't drink. Or shouldn't. Good night.

GEORGE: No, please stay. Please. *(His head stops bobbing. To* ANGEL*)* Just look at all the turmoil you create.

ANGEL: Who, me?

*(*GEORGE *leans in, takes* ANGEL'*s hand as* DEE *empties his drink.)*

GEORGE: Go easy with me, okay?

ANGEL: Now what fun would that be?

(Lights out on the quartet. Lights up on ANGEL *and* DEE, *who are walking.)*

DEE: Okay, why are we walking home when we could be in George Lanier's limo?

ANGEL: Did you see Cha Cha's face when I said, "no thanks, we'll walk"?

DEE: Chi Chi.

ANGEL: You have to always keep them guessing. George has everyone yessing him all day long, I say no and I become the last thing he thinks about when he goes to bed and the first thing he'll think about when he gets up. I get to make the rules and change the rules as we go along. Oh look. *(He points to the sidewalk.)* The sidewalk. Kind of glitters, doesn't it?

DEE: Glitter and be gay.

ANGEL: The first time we came to New York I thought there were little diamonds embedded in the sidewalks. I really did. I couldn't understand how no one else saw that. I was so angry when someone told me they were just glass particles. Where's the magic in that?

DEE: We were thirteen. Even then you could stop traffic. I wasn't far behind though, I could stop a clock.

(ANGEL *and* DEE *laugh.* ANGEL *takes off his [*DEE's*] coat and puts it around* DEE's *shoulders.*)

DEE: Aren't you cold?

ANGEL: Those were nice things you said about me to George.

DEE: All true.

ANGEL: I know. You always say nice things about me. Always.

DEE: Hey, when I broke my leg and missed so much school that I almost didn't graduate, who slept with the principal so I would get my diploma?

ANGEL: Like I would even consider graduating without my Dee. C'mon, you need your beauty sleep. You don't mind sleeping on the couch, do you? Of course you don't. ...Dee?

DEE: What baby?

ANGEL: Nothing. ...Don't let Danny split us up.

DEE: He won't.

ANGEL: Promise?

DEE: I promise.

ANGEL: ...I don't think I'd like to live in a world without you. I don't think I'd know how.

(*SIlence.* DEE *takes the coat off his shoulders, he helps* ANGEL *put one arm through one sleeve and then* DEE *puts his arm through the other sleeve, they are now both wearing the coat.*)

DEE: *(Sings)*
We're just two little boys from Little Rock

(ANGEL looks down. DEE takes ANGEL's hand and kisses it.)

ANGEL: *(Sings, softly at first)*
And we lived on the wrong side of the tracks

DEE: *(Sings)*
But the gentlemen who would come to call

ANGEL: *(Sings)*
They never did seem to mind at all

ANGEL & DEE: *(Sing)*
They came to the wrong side of the tracks

(ANGEL and DEE head off, holding hands as Marilyn Monroe's voice comes up as GEORGE's penthouse office slides in.)

ANGEL & DEE: *(Sing)*
Then someone broke my heart in Little Rock
So I up and left the pieces there
Like a little lost lamb I roamed about
I came to New York and I found out
That men are the same way everywhere

(Final drumbeats are repeated as DEE enters.)

VOICE: Mr Lanier will see you now.

(DEE looks around for the source of the voice, enters GEORGE's office.)

GEORGE: Thanks for coming.

DEE: Wow. This is some office.

GEORGE: You're impressed?

DEE: Who wouldn't be?

GEORGE: Angel calls it a work in progress. He wants me to go up a flight, make that wall all glass, so we can look out at our kingdom.

DEE: Did he say "our"?

GEORGE: Actually he said "his".

DEE: That's my boy.

(DEE *and* GEORGE *laugh.* GEORGE *concentrates very hard and his head stops bobbing.*)

GEORGE: Is my head bobbing?

DEE: Steady as Mount Rushmore. So what is it you do exactly?

GEORGE: I make money.

DEE: Print it up yourself, huh?

GEORGE: I have different holdings, corporations, patents, I could show you my portfolio.

DEE: Why sir, we hardly know each other. Well, whatever you're doing it's working. Boy, is it working.

GEORGE: Dee, this is a little awkward, but I just need to know, are you in love with Angel?

DEE: No. I have a lover and besides it's not that kind of love. It's, …Angel's my baby. I don't know how else to say it. We're the same age but I practically raised him. He sends me Mother's Day cards. Okay, I meant to keep that a secret.

GEORGE: Maybe you can help me then. I'm running out of ideas of what to get Angel. I've bought him everything I can think of, I've even got the staff working overtime, whoever comes up with the best idea for a gift wins a bonus; but they're drying out on me.

DEE: And after three weeks, imagine that. It's not hard. Just more. More of everything. …Give him an island. I don't think he's ever gotten one of those.

GEORGE: Manhattan it is.

(DEE *Laughs, then stops, stares at* GEORGE.)

DEE: You're not serious are you?

GEORGE: You win today's bonus.

DEE: What?

GEORGE: You win today's bonus. What do you want?

DEE: Me? Oh nothing, please.

GEORGE: Come on. Angel tells me I have a moral obligation to spend.

DEE: Moral obligation? Chi Chi must be rubbing off on him.

GEORGE: How about a job here? You can be in charge of all things Angel.

DEE: I already am.

(DEE senses GEORGE staring at him.)

DEE: What? Why are you staring? Do I have a pimple? I swear I felt it coming on this morning.

GEORGE: No. I'm just amazed how different you and Angel are.

DEE: Well, sure, he's perfect.

GEORGE: And you?

DEE: What's the opposite of perfect?

(ANGEL arrives in GEORGE's obviously oversized suit.)

ANGEL: Morning.

GEORGE: Speaking of the devil.

DEE: It's three P M.

ANGEL: *(Laserlike to GEORGE)* Good morning.

GEORGE: Good morning.

ANGEL: When I got up you were already gone, and I didn't like it. It surprised me how much I didn't like it. So I put on your clothes so I could pretend you were still with me.

DEE: I'll let myself out.

ANGEL: They smell like you.

(CHI CHI enters.)

CHI CHI: This is a check for the Community Center, ju gotta sign it. *(Takes in ANGEL's outfit)* Oh jello, little boy. Nothing in jour size today?

ANGEL: So I thought I should come here and give you your clothes back.

CHI CHI: I said I gotta check here. Jello.

GEORGE: Later.

(ANGEL takes off the suit jacket, smells it and drops it on the floor.)

ANGEL: You don't use cologne.

GEORGE: I'm allergic.

ANGEL: I like that you don't. This may take a while. You may want to sit down. *(He takes off his tie. After each item he takes off he either smells it tenderly or kisses it.)* Of course you'll have to get me something else to wear. I'm pretty sure that everything that I have on is yours.

(ANGEL takes off the shirt. GEORGE sits. CHI CHI goes towards GEORGE with the unsigned check but DEE stops him.)

DEE: Later.

CHI CHI: Ju ain't the boss of me.

(ANGEL whips off his belt, his pants immediately fall to his ankles. CHI CHI stares in spite of himself.)

CHI CHI: Later it is.

ANGEL: I can step right out of them. See?

(GEORGE nods as ANGEL steps out of his pants.)

CHI CHI: Oh great, now his head is bobbing again.

(ANGEL *begins to take off his tee shirt.*)

GEORGE: There are no curtains on these windows.

(DEE *and* CHI CHI *turn as one for the exit.* ANGEL *smiles.*)

ANGEL: I think these boxers are yours, too.

(DEE *and* CHI CHI *exit.* DEE *leaves,* CHI CHI *stays outside the door, after a beat opens the door again and sneaks a peek. He stares as* ANGEL *goes to* GEORGE. ANGEL *takes off his boxers.* CHI CHI *closes the door and exits.*)

ANGEL: May I sit in your chair?

(GEORGE *gets up,* ANGEL *sits, feeling the arm rests and head rest. he luxuriates in them. he turns the chair around looking out at the view.* GEORGE *comes up behind him in the chair.* ANGEL *takes his hand and kisses it,* GEORGE *kisses the top of* ANGEL's *head.*)

GEORGE: Oh Angel.

ANGEL: Oh George. ...Let's go shopping.

(*Music: a song like Ella Fitzgerald, "I'll Take Manhattan." Song bleeds into sounds of cash registers going crazy. Shopping. An impossibly expensive store.* GRETCHEN *darts in, carrying some men's pajamas. She is pursued by a hissing* BREE.)

BREE: Gretchen!

GRETCHEN: Leave me alone!

BREE: Gretchen!

GRETCHEN: Leave me alone!

BREE: Have you lost the one iota of pride you had left? Let's just get the word "doormat" tattooed on your forehead.

GRETCHEN: Seth needs these.

BREE: He most certainly does *not* need silk pajamas.

GRETCHEN: He showed me what the state issued him—

BREE: You're visiting him?!

GRETCHEN: So rough and coarse against his delicate skin.

BREE: Will you listen to yourself?

GRETCHEN: How are we as a caring society supposed to rehabilitate anyone if they can't get a good night's sleep. Now I ask you.

BREE: We don't want them rehabilitated. Rehabilitation is the last thing on our mind.

GRETCHEN: Seth cried. My Seth cried. He told me he was sorry if he hurt me.

BREE: I believe he offered the same generic apology to the stockholders.

GRETCHEN: He said that he misses me.

BREE: The only thing that son of a bitch misses is what his life was like before he was caught. Put back the pajamas.

GRETCHEN: They're blue. They match his eyes.

BREE: And I can guarantee you that if I asked him what color your eyes were he wouldn't know.

GRETCHEN: Don't you miss Fletcher? Even a little bit?

BREE: Hell no! *(She takes one of the legs of the pajamas.)* Now, hold on to the other end, and pull.

GRETCHEN: I can't!

BREE: Pull damn it!

(BREE and GRETCHEN begin to pull the pajamas apart at the crotch.)

BREE: Pull for all the lies. Pull for all the times he broke your heart! Pull because if you don't pull you'll go insane!!

(The pajamas split in half. BREE *and* GRETCHEN *are gasping for air as a* SALESPERSON *hurries in.)*

SALESPERSON: Excuse me, madam…?

BREE: Don't pop a blood vessel, we're buying it. Here. *(She gives him the pajama top.)* Take this top and split it in half, too. And we'll need each half wrapped in two separate lovely gift boxes. Thank you so very much.

(A confused SALESPERSON *exits with the pajamas.)*

BREE: I think we're being more than generous, don't you? Now what say we do a little shopping? For us.

GRETCHEN: But only things we absolutely, positively need.

BREE: Of course. Let's start at the fur salon.

GRETCHEN: Right behind you.

*(*BREE *and* GRETCHEN *exit. Enter a blissful* ANGEL *and* GEORGE *followed by* DEE *and* CHI CHI.*)*

GEORGE: Now I want you pick anything you want, as much as you want. Go back for seconds, thirds, hell, buy out the entire inventory of anything that strikes your fancy. If it makes you smile, it's yours.

*(*ANGEL *and* GEORGE *kiss passionately.)*

CHI CHI: Get a room.

*(*SALESPERSON *enters.)*

SALESPERSON: Excuse me?

GEORGE: *(Still lost in* ANGEL.*)* George Lanier.

SALESPERSON: How lovely for you.

CHI CHI: As in George Lanier who owns the building jou're in, the block it's on and the city's it's in.

SALESPERSON: Why, Mr Lanier, of course. What a pleasure.

GEORGE: This, young man, this Angel, is going to be doing some shopping here. It may be one item or it could be the entire store, that's really up to him. And when it comes to him, money is no object. He can have anything he wants. I'll wait right here while this store becomes his personal sandbox. Any questions?

(SALESPERSON *shakes his head.*)

GEORGE: You work on commission don't you?

(SALESPERSON *nods his head.*)

GEORGE: Then you are a very lucky man. (*To* ANGEL) Go play.

ANGEL: I hope I find something I like.

(ANGEL *and* GEORGE *kiss.*)

ANGEL: I promise to try really hard. Come on, Dee. Maybe we can find something to disguise that sallow complexion of yours.

(ANGEL *and* DEE *exit.* GEORGE *looks after them, sighs.*)

GEORGE: Ask me how the morning wood is.

CHI CHI: Oh God, do I have to?

GEORGE: I'm tenting out right now! I'm talking morning wood, mid afternoon wood, three times in the evening wood—

CHI CHI: Okay, baby, jour happy, good for ju.

GEORGE: No, no, see it's more than that. He's like a jolt of electricity to me.

CHI CHI: Oh jeah, little puta boy is wonderful.

GEORGE: Why do you want to ruin this for me? Could you maybe pretend to be happy for me? Is it too much to ask that the person who I consider my friend, be happy for me? I'm in—

(CHI CHI *jumps in, not letting* GEORGE *finish.*)

CHI CHI: Don't say it! Please. Jeah, okay. Give Angel anything he wants. Have fun, go crazy, go nuts, just don't give him jour heart, that's all.

GEORGE: Tell you what, whatever he spends today I'll send the same amount to any organization you choose. In fact, I'll double it.

CHI CHI: It's not always about the money. Jou're a role model now, ju gotta represent, the gay jouth looks up to ju, ju can't be trifling with Mr Cash and Carry.

GEORGE: Could you not call him that? Don't you want me to be happy?

CHI CHI: Sure. Just not stupid happy.

(A dismayed CHI CHI *exits as we come up on* ANGEL, DEE *and the* SALESPERSON.*)*

ANGEL: May I have that sweater, please.

SALESPERSON: Of course. We have it in many other colors.

ANGEL: Oh. Then I'd like all of them. And every size. Please. *(Wanting to share his joy with* DEE.*)* That way no one else will have my sweater.

*(*DEE *is silent.)*

ANGEL: Won't that be fun? Dee? ...I don't think my Dee approves. I think I'd like one for my friend, too.

DEE: No, that's okay.

ANGEL: Then we'll be the only two people in the city with the sweater. We'll be like a club.

*(*SALESPERSON *is about to exit.)*

ANGEL: He's hard to fit, but I don't have to tell you that.

*(*SALESPERSON *exits.)*

ANGEL: Is my little Dee sad? Now there must be something in this great big store that will bring a smile to your face.

DEE: I think he's in love with you.

ANGEL: Well, of course he is. *(Pointing to a shirt)* What do you think?

DEE: No, I mean really in love with you.

ANGEL: *(As if to a child)* I know. Let's go upstairs.

DEE: How do you feel about him? He's a nice guy. Really nice.

(ANGEL nods. Where is this conversation going?)

DEE: I mean, I don't think he's like the others.

ANGEL: He's exactly like the others.

DEE: He sees you and he lights up. The man glows when you walk into a room.

ANGEL: You're my best friend in the whole entire world and you know why? Because you love me no matter what. And I love you, with all your faults. I wouldn't trade what we have for anything in the world. So don't worry, he's not going to take your place. George is a temporary distraction and I'll leave him before he can ever tire of me. Not that he ever would. Now, you go find something ridiculously overpriced, something that will make Chi Chi cringe when he sees the price tag.

DEE: I don't think George is going to tire of you.

ANGEL: I know that! Didn't I just say that?

DEE: No, you said you wanted to leave before he did.

ANGEL: Don't make me forget I like you, Dee.

(ANGEL heads out as DEE stares after him. DEE tries to exit the store. GEORGE's head is bobbing, but less so than earlier.)

GEORGE: You're not trying to leave without me buying you some happiness, are you?

DEE: I'm not much of a shopper.

GEORGE: It's not that hard. Or so Angel tells me.

DEE: I already like you, George, you don't have to buy me anything.

GEORGE: I know I don't have to. I want to.

DEE: Okay, when was the last time you bought yourself something?

GEORGE: Well, you can't go by me.

DEE: Thought so.

GEORGE: You shouldn't hold my money against me.

DEE: How's that again?

GEORGE: I just don't want you to feel uncomfortable, that's all. I mean, I wasn't born rich.

DEE: No. Just lucky. And handsome. And sweet. Okay, shoot me now.

GEORGE: Let me tell you a little story about my mother. Single, no family, no anybody but me. She had to take three buses to get to work. Took her two and a half hours, each way. She'd get up at five A M, leave me my food and set the alarm for me so I wouldn't miss school. I was always cutting classes though, got teased an awful lot cause of my head bobbing all the time. You know how cruel kids can be.

DEE: So they tell me.

GEORGE: One day I got up, right after she left and I went to the window, it was snowing. And I saw this little figure, walking in the snow, to the bus stop. She waited there in her cloth coat and kerchief on her head. Waited in the snow, then got on the bus and was gone. You see something like that, that kind of sacrifice and it

changes you. I never missed school again, I didn't care
what the kids did to me or said to me, cause as hard as
my life was, and it was, it was harder for my mother.

DEE: I'm sure she's very proud of you.

GEORGE: Was. She passed away about ten years ago.
I really didn't make much money until a year before
she died. Then whoosh! All of a sudden I'm richer than
most small countries.

DEE: At least she got to see it.

GEORGE: You know what she would love? When I
would give her checks. Wouldn't cash them, just put
them away in a box, take them out every so often and
look at them. Spread them on the table, the bed, the
floor. Just this whole army of checks.

DEE: She never cashed them?

GEORGE: Nah. *(Silence. He laughs to himself.)* Angel
would have cashed them.

DEE: In a heartbeat. Hello.

GEORGE: I wish she would have. I wish Angel could
have taught her how to enjoy it. She was always kind
of afraid of my money, made me kind of afraid of it,
too. I love how Angel just takes it for granted that there
will always be money there when he needs it. There's
so little joy in the world, why not grab it? *(His head
bobbing more noticeably)* Do you think Angel likes me? I
mean, really likes me?

DEE: *(Laughs)* What are we, like twelve? Oh, he has like
a mad crush on you, girl. *(Sees that GEORGE is serious.)*
Of course he does. I mean, come on, how could he not?

*(CHI CHI stops SALESPERSON wheeling a full clothing rack
of potential ANGEL wear.)*

CHI CHI: Excuse me, what's this?

SALESPERSON: I'm terrible sorry, but these items are spoken for. They're for, well, he's having me call him Angel.

CHI CHI: Please, Mr Puta to ju.

SALESPERSON: And you would be…?

CHI CHI: His stylist.

SALESPERSON: Oh. Of course.

(CHI CHI *looks through the rack.*)

CHI CHI: Hate it. Hate it. Hate it enough to kill. What? No spandex or mesh?

SALESPERSON: I don't believe we carry any.

CHI CHI: *(Indicating for the* SALESPERSON *to lean in for the real 411.)* Well, just between ju and me and the four walls, that's where all the big money goes, ju know what I'm saying, Mr Work on Commission.?

(SALESPERSON *has a beat to register this new information then takes off in hot pursuit of those items, nods to* ANGEL *as he exits.)*

SALESPERSON: I'll be right back, Mr Puta.

(ANGEL *looks at* CHI CHI.)

ANGEL: This from a man named after a gay porn director. *(He begins to look through the rack.)* You should pick something. A little peace offering from me to you.

CHI CHI: Ju mean from George. No thanks.

ANGEL: You don't like me, do you?

CHI CHI: Wait a second, let me put my surprised face on. No. I don't like ju. I hate ju. And everything about ju.

ANGEL: I don't hate anybody. *(Thinks for a second.)* Nope. I don't. Weren't the sixties supposed to be all about peace and love? *(He goes behind the rack.)*

CHI CHI: Okay, bottom line it for me, how much will it cost to get rid of ju? Give me a dollar amount. I'll get it for ju.

(ANGEL *has taken off his pants, flops them over the rack. He walks around to the front of the rack in his underwear, looking through the clothes.*)

CHI CHI: Before ju break his heart.

(ANGEL *holds up a pair of trousers.*)

ANGEL: What do you think of these? I like them. *(He takes them and heads behind the rack to put them on.)* No peeking.

CHI CHI: Ju wish.

ANGEL: Like last time in the office. I saw your reflection in the window when you came back to look at me. Are you blushing, Chi Chi? Oh yeah, you would have given anything to trade places with George just for that one moment. Not for his money, but for me. You wanted me. *(Steps around the rack to the front, now wearing the trousers.)* It's okay, I get that a lot. I can bring a room to its knees, literally and figuratively, silence it with just a hint of a smile and destroy somebody by screening my phone calls.

CHI CHI: Just imagine what ju could do if ju actually had a heart.

ANGEL: I have a heart. It's just a practical one.

CHI CHI: All this power ju think ju have, it has an expiration date on it, ju know that, right? Trophy boy, trophy man, no such thing as trophy geezer. So, how old are ju?

(ANGEL *stops rifling through the rack.*)

CHI CHI: That old, huh?

(CHI CHI *tsks tsks as he exits. Back to* GEORGE *and* DEE.*)

GEORGE: You can't leave, not like this. You are forcing my hand.

DEE: What? What do you mean?

(GEORGE *picks up* DEE *and slings him over his shoulder.*)

GEORGE: I'm buying you something.

DEE: Whoa. Okay, not a wise move.

GEORGE: It's what my Angel wants. And what Angel wants, Angel gets.

DEE: *(Laughing)* You're insane.

GEORGE: You are going shopping young man.

DEE: You're going to kill yourself. Me. On the floor. Now.

(GEORGE *playfully slaps* DEE *on the butt, spins him around.*)

GEORGE: Okay, which way? Let's start with summer suits. Though why anyone would want to wear a suit in the summer I don't know.

DEE: You got me.

GEORGE: *(Laughs)* Yep, I sure do, don't I?

(CHI CHI *enters.*)

CHI CHI: Jello, is this the Pleasure Chest?

(GEORGE *puts* DEE *down, both are sheepish.*)

GEORGE: No, no, this isn't what it looks like, you see, Dee didn't want to go shopping.

DEE: No, I certainly didn't, and George, you know, was just, well, you know…

CHI CHI: Giving ju a pony ride? That's so cute.

DEE: I think I'll, uh, go find Angel. He's probably looking for me. *(He exits.)*

GEORGE: …I'm a little out of breath.

CHI CHI: Uh huh.

GEORGE: Should be working out more, I guess.

CHI CHI: Uh huh. Tell me, what time is it?

GEORGE: Five P M.

CHI CHI: P M, huh, Strange, both ju and Dee had some major morning wood going on back there, ju know what I'm saying?

(GEORGE turns to check himself. DEE arrives to see ANGEL throw one garment after another on the floor.)

ANGEL: Thank goodness you're here. I've decided not to get a thing. I think George needs to take me shopping in Paris, what do you think?

(DEE is silent.)

ANGEL: Yeah, you're right. They have some nice things here, but they're so common, you know? Pretentious rich people clothing. Though it would be kind of fun having six people following me down the street, all carrying bags of stuff for me and everybody staring at me and you have got to say something. *(Silence)* Say something. He would buy me anything, wouldn't he?

(DEE starts to pick up some of the clothing that has fallen off the rack and put them back on their hangers. ANGEL knocks them out of his hands.)

ANGEL: You know something. What is it?

(GRETCHEN and BREE enter.)

GRETCHEN: Well, look what the cat dragged in.

BREE: Face first.

GRETCHEN: Zing!

ANGEL: Aren't there supposed to be three ugly witches in *Macbeth*?

BREE: It reads.

GRETCHEN: Imagine that.

BREE: Nice to see you landed on your feet.

GRETCHEN: For a change.

BREE: Now be a good worker drone and fetch me this in a moss green.

GRETCHEN: Chop chop.

BREE: Before I have you fired.

GRETCHEN: Oh, who are we kidding? We're going to have him fired anyway.

ANGEL: Actually, ladies, I'm here as a customer.

GRETCHEN: Did we somehow enter a Dollar Store?

BREE: Who knows, after that fifth cocktail my sense of direction is shot.

ANGEL: Speaking of shot, how is Seth?

GRETCHEN: Why you little—

(BREE *holds back* GRETCHEN.)

BREE: Easy cowgirl.

ANGEL: You're both alone, but I'm not surprised. I'm here with George. As in Lanier.

(DEE *turns to leave,* ANGEL *grabs his hand to stop him from leaving while never taking his eyes off* GRETCHEN *and* BREE.)

ANGEL: You know him, the man who can buy and sell you. That's what I'll have him buy me! You're company. Christie Industries with a nice red bow on it. What do you think, Dee?

BREE: Maybe he'll even put it in your name, so you're not just the hired help anymore.

(GEORGE *and* CHI CHI *enter.*)

GRETCHEN: So easily replaceable.

BREE: And forgettable.

GEORGE: Angel…?

GRETCHEN: Don't let the name fool you. Excuse us, Mr Lanier.

BREE: As always a pleasure.

GEORGE: Is there something wrong? What were you saying to my Angel?

GRETCHEN: Your Angel?

BREE: It is to guffaw.

GRETCHEN: Yours until he finds someone richer.

GEORGE: I think you need to apologize to him. And to me.

GRETCHEN: First ask him if you're the first rich man he's lead around on a penis leash.

BREE: Gretchen!

GEORGE: All I know is that I love him and I hope that he loves me.

BREE: Gretchen, come along. There's a lovely cocktail calling out your name.

GRETCHEN: Don't you dare use that word! You boys play at love but come back to me when you've earned it. When you stand by each other in sickness and in health and you can't imagine your life without him. When you wake up in the middle of the night just to look at him. When you hang in there no matter how hard it gets or how much people laugh behind your back and you still can't stop loving him.

CHI CHI: Meltdown on aisle six.

GRETCHEN: When even your friends and your family drop you, drop you as if you didn't exist anymore and all you have to go on are the fumes, the goddamn embers of what you feel for him, cause it won't die out,

ACT ONE

it just *won't!*, then and only then can you talk to me about love!

BREE: ...She's a tad upset, Mr Lanier, not at you, of course, but at that... *(She points to* ANGEL.*)* ...thing.

GEORGE: The man I love.

BREE & CHI CHI: Oh please.

GEORGE: You can't put your love up on a pedestal while you knock mine down. My love means as much to me as yours does to you. *(He looks around, sees that* DEE *is wearing a ring.)* Dee, may I borrow your ring? *(His head bobbing, he takes the ring off* DEE's *hand and goes down on one knee before* ANGEL.*)* I love you, Angel. I do. I know this is sudden, but would you do me the great honor, would you, will you marry me?

ANGEL: Me? Yes, yes, sweet Jesus, of course I'll marry you!

*(*ANGEL *embraces* GEORGE, *looks over his shoulder to a stunned* DEE.*)*

ANGEL: Jackpot!

END OF ACT ONE

ACT TWO

*(Suggested song: The Dixie Cups, "Goin to the Chapel."
Amid a flurry of flashbulbs lights slowly come up on a
podium. A somber* CHI CHI, *think Edwardian velvet with a
turtleneck, enters the stage.)*

VOICE: Mr Chi Chi Lopez will now answer questions
from the ladies and gentlemen of the press.

(All of the REPORTERS *questions come from off stage. Great
to have as many* REPORTERS *as possible.)*

REPORTER: Chi Chi, over here, Chi Chi—

REPORTER: Where did they meet, Chi Chi?

CHI CHI: George met his true love at an orphanage
where Angel was reading to the blind. Although if it
was Tuesday he could have been donating blood. It's
so hard to keep up with all his charitable work. Angel
is such a giver.

REPORTER: What's Angel's last name?

CHI CHI: What do ju care, it's gonna be Lanier in a
couple of weeks.

REPORTER: Chi Chi, over here—

REPORTER: Mr Lopez—

CHI CHI: Hey, let's keep it orderly people. This is not
the White House. *(To A* REPORTER*)* Hey don't I know ju
from an adults only website?

REPORTER: Why not just a civil union?

CHI CHI: I don't know. Why didn't jour parents just have a civil union? George Lanier didn't check a box that said "unequal" to straights on his tax return, okay?

REPORTER: What do you say to those persistent rumors that Angel is nothing more than a gold digger out to fleece George Lanier?

CHI CHI: Ju don't wanna know what I have to say.

REPORTER: Will there be a prenup?

CHI CHI: I'm happy to say "no", because those two crazy kids are so much in love.

REPORTER: Won't their marriage be illegal?

CHI CHI: So is taxation without representation.

REPORTER: No it isn't.

REPORTER: That's perfectly legal.

CHI CHI: Don't even start with me, cause I don't play. If gay people pay taxes they have the same rights as any tax payer. Don't forget that when King George wanted ju to pay taxes without any representation in the English Parliament, all of a sudden the American Revolution seemed like a fab idea. This country was built on civil disobedience. Learn jour history. Every time there's been a change in society people have fought it tooth and Lee press on nail. With liberty and justice for all, remember that, pendejo? I want ju people to remember that what others take for granted, we honor. George Lanier is a wonderful, wonderful man and Angel, well Angel is a little piece of heaven here on earth.

REPORTER: Chi Chi, over here—

REPORTER: Chi Chi—

(Lights shift to GEORGE's *office, where* ANGEL *and* DEE *are looking over the newspapers.* ANGEL *happily spins around in the chair.)*

ANGEL: They Sally Field me!! Everybody's writing such beautiful things about me.

DEE: *(Reading)* When did you ever work in a soup kitchen?

ANGEL: So not the point. Chi Chi is giving them an overall view of me. The true essence of what is Angel. Last night, George and I went out to dinner and people stood up and applauded.

DEE: Yeah, but this Angel that Chi Chi is creating isn't you.

ANGEL: I would do volunteer work, feed the blind, read to the homeless, enable the environment, if I had any free time. It's a full time job being me. Fashion week is coming up and I've been invited to every show, and there are just so many hours in the day.

(CHI CHI enters.)

ANGEL: And there's my little P R P R.

(CHI CHI goes straight to the office bar, takes a bottle and drinks directly from it.)

ANGEL: Rough day at the salt mines?

CHI CHI: Lissen you little Skanks R Us, I have spent the last forty eight hours creating a person who doesn't exist, giving a soul to the soul less, a heart to the heart less, to ju who thinks Hetrick-Martin is the act Dean Martin had after he broke up with Jerry Lewis—

ANGEL: Who's Dean Martin?

CHI CHI: I had to make ju a role model. I had to build ju from the ground up. I had to make ju into Sidney Fucking Poitier in Guess Who's Coming to Dinner!

ANGEL: Is that his real name?

CHI CHI: People are waiting in line to say we don't deserve to get married, so I had to make ju worthy,

I had to make ju somebody George W would say deserved to marry the man he loves!

ANGEL: Dee, he's yelling at me.

CHI CHI: And that's who jou're going to be from now on, do ju hear me? Ju are going to be the role model every little gay boy and girl can look up to or as God is my witness I'll—

DEE: Angel never asked you to lie.

CHI CHI: Oh jeah, like I could sell the real him.

DEE: Angel is a wonderful person, with feelings—

CHI CHI: Everybody has feelings, but lemme tell ju something, that boy has never shed a tear for anybody but himself and that don't count! So, ju got jourself a George Lanier, congratulations, but ju also got jourself a Chi Chi Lopez, and that's not gonna be no party, baby!

(GEORGE *enters, with briefcase.*)

GEORGE: There's my Angel! …Is everything okay?

DEE: Everything's fine, George. Really.

GEORGE: (*To* ANGEL) It suddenly occurred to me that I owe my Angel something.

ANGEL: Chi Chi's resignation?

CHI CHI: Shut up, ca-ching, ca-ching.

DEE: Now boys.

GEORGE: (*To* ANGEL) No. There is still the matter of a ring of your very own, young man. So…

(GEORGE *opens the briefcase which is filled with a dazzling array of rings in every size and shape.* DEE *whistles.* ANGEL *begins to finger the ring he is already wearing.*)

DEE: Wow….

CHI CHI: (*Disapprovingly*) Jou're telling me.

GEORGE: Now, knowing my Angel the way I do, I'm guessing he's going to look at all this and say…

CHI CHI: *(Imitating* ANGEL*)* I'd like them all. Please.

GEORGE: And of course you can have every last one of them.

ANGEL: …They're beautiful…they really are, but…if it's okay, I'd like to keep this one. Please. *(He holds up his hand with* DEE's *simple gold band on it.)*

GEORGE: What?

CHI CHI: What?

ANGEL: I want this one. Please.

GEORGE: That was just a temporary one, Angel. That belongs to Dee. I borrowed it from him. It's probably the one Danny gave him when they first got together.

ANGEL: Dee won't mind. *(To* DEE*)* Will you? *(Back to* GEORGE *without waiting for* DEE's *response.)* See? Dee's okay with it. Please.

DEE: You can have the ring, Angel.

CHI CHI: Wait a second, jour man gave ju that ring and ju just giving it away? Oh honey, I'd smack ju.

*(*ANGEL *takes the briefcase full of rings and gives it to* DEE.*)*

ANGEL: Here. Then you take this. *(To* GEORGE*)* Okay? Okay? Please?

GEORGE: All you want is a simple gold band?

*(*ANGEL *nods.* GEORGE *kisses* ANGEL, CHI CHI *looks at* DEE *taking in the kiss.* DEE *closes the briefcase.)*

GEORGE: I can't deny you anything.

CHI CHI: Jeah that was so very sweet. Okay, here's jour prenup.

*(*CHI CHI *hands a contract to* GEORGE *who is still lost in* ANGEL.*)*

GEORGE: We're not doing a prenup, remember?

CHI CHI: That was just for the press, of course we're doing a prenup.

(GEORGE *tears up the prenup.*)

GEORGE: This is going to be my first and my last marriage. No need for this.

(ANGEL *smiles at* CHI CHI.)

CHI CHI: Can I see ju outside.

(ANGEL *and* GEORGE *kiss again.*)

GEORGE: No.

CHI CHI: Jou're late for something. I'm so sure of it.

GEORGE: It can wait.

ANGEL: Go ahead.

GEORGE: You'll be here when I get back?

ANGEL: Right here.

(*Before* GEORGE *leaves he takes* ANGEL's *hand, looks at the ring on it. He kisses* ANGEL's *hand. While* GEORGE *does this* DEE *gives the briefcase back to* CHI CHI.)

CHI CHI: Jour friend gave it to ju. It's jours.

DEE: It's not his to give and it's not mine to take.

(GEORGE *and* CHI CHI *exit,* GEORGE *barely able to take his eyes off* ANGEL. *Outside.* GEORGE *and* CHI CHI *head for the elevator.* GEORGE *puts up his hand to silence* CHI CHI *before he can say anything. They get on the elevator.*)

GEORGE: Okay, before you explode, you get to say one thing about the prenup and that's it. After that it's off limits. One thing. So make it count.

(*Beat.* CHI CHI *smacks the back of* GEORGE's *head. The elevator doors close. Back to* ANGEL *and* DEE.)

ANGEL: Where's the briefcase?

DEE: I gave it back.

ANGEL: Oh Dee, what am I going to do with you?

DEE: ...Why did you want my ring?

(ANGEL *looks at* DEE, *smiles.*)

ANGEL: Come here.

(DEE *sits next to* ANGEL.)

ANGEL: I wanted the ring because it came from you. Silly, isn't it? (*He puts his feet up on the couch and his head in* DEE's *lap.*) My Dee. ...You know, I always thought it'd be you.

DEE: Me what?

ANGEL: After I had all the money in the world, all the presents, that you and me would wind up together.

DEE: Yeah?

ANGEL: No sex of course, but like friends, you know?

DEE: I'll always be there for you, Angel.

ANGEL: I know. ...I don't like sharing you with what's his name? Darrin?

DEE: Danny.

(ANGEL *and* DEE *laugh gently.*)

DEE: Darrin.

ANGEL: Promise me when you're old it'll just be us two.

DEE: Angel...

ANGEL: I'll take that as a yes. Chi Chi doesn't like me. Too bad. I'm not going to change. I hate change. I don't want you to ever change and I'll never change. I'll always be the same Angel. I promise.

(DEE *gently kisses* ANGEL *on his head.*)

DEE: Do you love him?

(ANGEL looks up at DEE, his head in his lap.)

DEE: He's a really wonderful man.

ANGEL: Who wouldn't love being married to George Lanier? I mean come on, he's rich.

DEE: And he's sweet and when he talks to you, he looks right at you, and sometimes, when he's thinking about something, he hums. Doesn't even know he's doing it, just hums. It's kinda cute, isn't it?

ANGEL: And he's rich, why do you keep leaving out the most important part? He's the cutest billionaire I know.

DEE: So you do love him?

ANGEL: You know, I think I do. No, really. I love George Lanier.

(Back to GEORGE and CHI CHI.)

GEORGE: When those women started attacking him, I couldn't stand it, I got caught up in the moment. He just looked so vulnerable.

CHI CHI: Yeah, like a machete. Baby, jou're so not in love with Angel.

GEORGE: Maybe I am.

CHI CHI: No maybe about it, trust me, jou'll know when jou're in love.

GEORGE: I'm happier with Angel than I've ever been with anybody.

CHI CHI: Look, ju just came out. Ju don't marry the first man that makes ju smile.

GEORGE: Sometimes you're just ready to settle down. I am not a bar guy, I never was. I don't want a different guy every night of the week. I want one. That's all I've ever wanted.

CHI CHI: Jeah, but does it have to be him?

GEORGE: He's someone I can take care of. He needs me. This is who I want to spend my life with and it's my life, Chi Chi.

CHI CHI: Jeah, I know. Man, I wish ju would have gotten laid a whole lot more when ju were growing up. Ju'd know there's a lot of men out there who could make ju smile. Smile hell, they'd curl jour toes.

GEORGE: Well, I never met them—

CHI CHI: Man, you gotta give jourself a little chance for romance.

GEORGE: I wish I could be romantic. Maybe I could learn.

CHI CHI: Not ju! The other guy! Oh, what the hell!

(CHI CHI *suddenly kisses* GEORGE. *Deeply, passionately. They break apart, look at each other for a second, each trying to evaluate their response to the kiss. It's like kissing cardboard.*)

CHI CHI: Nothing.

GEORGE: You're telling me.

CHI CHI: Hey!

(CHI CHI *hits* GEORGE *playfully with the briefcase.*)

GEORGE: What are you doing with that? I thought Angel gave those rings to Dee.

CHI CHI: He did, but Dee turned them down. Not everybody's for sale, ju know.

GEORGE: Angel is not for sale.

CHI CHI: Who said he was? So sensitive. Omigod, I betcho Dee doesn't jell at Angel like that.

GEORGE: I wasn't yelling.

CHI CHI: Dee is always so nice to Angel.

GEORGE: That's because Dee is perfect.

CHI CHI: What ju say?

(Elevator ding)

CHI CHI: Oh, look, our floor.

(Enter GRETCHEN, *toting a leopard print clutch and wearing a wedding dress.)*

GRETCHEN: Ready for drinks at the Plaza.

BREE: Gretchen, uh, Gretchen, dearest…

GRETCHEN: Then I thought we'd hit Le Cirque for dinner. Or maybe the Four Seasons. Show the world we're still a force to be reckoned with.

BREE: Looked at a calendar recently? It's after Labor day.

GRETCHEN: *(Pointing to her dress)* Oh, you mean this?

BREE: That's precisely what I mean.

GRETCHEN: This is my very visual protest to George Lanier's wedding to Satan.

BREE: Angel.

GRETCHEN: Don't correct me when I'm right.

BREE: You're planning on wearing that out in public?

GRETCHEN: Yes. To illustrate what a true bride should look like.

BREE: As if we weren't already social outcasts.

GRETCHEN: Help me with my veil.

*(*BREE *does, takes a step back.)*

BREE: You look…stunning.

GRETCHEN: Do I?

BREE: No, of course not, you look like an absolute idiot, but hey, we're all we've got.

GRETCHEN: So you'll stand by my homage to traditional values?

BREE: What the hell, as long as you don't spill your drink.

GRETCHEN: And I plan on wearing my wedding dress every day until that sham of a marriage is called off.

BREE: Your wedding dress?

GRETCHEN: Yes, my wedding dress.

BREE: In what parallel universe did you wear white?

GRETCHEN: Grab my train.

(BREE *does.*)

BREE: You could have at least gone with a nice pastel.

GRETCHEN: Seth wore lilac to our wedding.

BREE: Not many men can carry a lilac tuxedo.

GRETCHEN: ...It was a jumpsuit.

BREE: And yet somehow the entire Angel episode came as a complete surprise to you.

GRETCHEN: Didn't Fletcher have a jumpsuit?

BREE: ...Canary yellow. Whatever you do, do not let me stop drinking tonight.

(*As* BREE *and* GRETCHEN *exit:*)

GRETCHEN: Did I mentioned we honeymooned in San Francisco?

(*A song like RuPaul's "Supermodel" blares as* ANGEL *and* CHI CHI *arrive at a hospice kitchen. Music slowly fades.*)

ANGEL: I can't believe you scheduled a seven A M photo shoot. Where's Annie Lebowitz?

CHI CHI: Probably at home in bed. Lissen—

ANGEL: What?!

CHI CHI: Put on this apron.

ANGEL: You're insane! White? Under over head lighting?

(CHI CHI *is putting the apron on* ANGEL.)

ANGEL: Get me something in a teal at least.

CHI CHI: Jou're gonna start packing up these meals, the press is going to arrive and take jour picture and follow on a full day with ju—

ANGEL: Oh, the press!

CHI CHI: That's right, puta boy, the press. After delivering breakfast to P W A they're gonna follow ju to a homeless shelter where jou're gonna make the beds—

ANGEL: How can they have beds if they're homeless?

CHI CHI: From there jou'll all take the cross town subway—

ANGEL: Oh, I'm sorry, I don't do subways.

CHI CHI: To a junior high in Hell's Kitchen where jou're gonna talk to the kids about tolerance. Here's jour speech, ju can learn it on the subway.

ANGEL: Again with the subway.

CHI CHI: After that there's a demonstration at the U N protesting the U S not signing the Kyoto treaty. Then jou're off to a community center in Alphabet City where jou're gonna play dominoes with the elderly.

ANGEL: I draw the line at dominoes!

CHI CHI: Or read to them, or just listen to them, whatever. Ju are there to serve them. (*He hands him a chef's hat.*) Put the hat on.

(*No response*)

CHI CHI: Put the —

ANGEL: Listen here, J.Lo, I let you go on because I wanted to see just what kind of sadist you are.

CHI CHI: Put the hat on.

ANGEL: I'm not putting the hat on, I'm not taking
the subway and I'm not playing dominoes with the
Depends crowd, got that? You call me when it's a
Vanity Fair cover shoot and not a second before. *(About
to take off his apron.)*

CHI CHI: Until ju marry George, I own ju. All that press
jou're so crazy about, I control it, I spin it. Ju want to
see just how fast I can destroy ju? How quickly I can
make ju the laughing stock of New York and persona
non grata at every social event in the city? I control
everyday of jour life until that ring is on jour finger,
capiche? Now put on the goddamn hat, *puta* boy.

(Beat. ANGEL *puts on the hat.)*

CHI CHI: Smile, baby, here comes the press.

ANGEL: Someday you will pay for having offended
Don Coreleone.

*(*ANGEL *smiles for the camera. Lights out on them as we go
to* DEE *who opens his door to* GEORGE.*)*

DEE: What are you doing here?

GEORGE: …I've left you without a ring.

DEE: I said it was okay.

GEORGE: No, it's unacceptable. I should really
apologize to Danny.

DEE: Just missed him. They called him to sub for
another pilot. He could be anywhere.

GEORGE: I was looking forward to maybe finally
meeting him.

DEE: Angel calls him Dolly Parton's husband. You
know he's out there you just never see him.

GEORGE: Can I come in?

DEE: Oh, I'm sorry. Sure.

GEORGE: It was very nice of you to give up your ring.

DEE: Whatever makes Angel happy, right? Drink?

GEORGE: I don't, uh—

DEE: Oh, that's right, you don't.

GEORGE: But you go ahead, please.

DEE: No, I'm fine.

GEORGE: What airline does Danny work for?

DEE: I think I will have a little drink. *(He prepares himself a drink.)* I can't tell you that, because knowing you, you'd buy him the airline.

GEORGE: Any pictures?

DEE: Just one. He hates having his picture taken.

(DEE shows GEORGE a framed photo.)

GEORGE: Very attractive.

DEE: Yeah. *(He makes a big show of kissing the picture.)*

GEORGE: Where'd you two meet?

DEE: At a bar. I hate bars. No one looks at you, or I should say, me. Unless I come in with Angel. But I was alone, and Danny just looked at me and you know how you look at somebody sometimes and there's this flash of recognition. Not like, I know you, but more like, I'm going to know you. And it's going to matter that I know you.

GEORGE: How did you know Danny was the one?

DEE: I guess I didn't feel alone anymore.

GEORGE: Is he romantic?

DEE: Oh boy, is he.

GEORGE: I wish I were.

DEE: Are you kidding? You're always buying Angel things.

(GEORGE's head begins to bob.)

GEORGE: People have always bought him things. I want to be different from the rest. Do something for him that he won't expect. ...Could I ask you for a favor?

DEE: Sure.

GEORGE: I want to write a toast to Angel for our wedding and no one knows him better than you do, maybe, if you're not too busy, you could help me with it.

DEE: Well, I guess better me than Chi Chi.

(DEE and GEORGE laugh.)

GEORGE: Could you imagine what kind of toast that would be? So, tell me everything you know about my Angel.

DEE: Well, he's gorgeous.

GEORGE: Check.

DEE: And, sexy.

GEORGE: Don't have to tell me.

DEE: And...

GEORGE: Brutally honest.

DEE: See? You are good at this game.

(DEE and GEORGE laugh.)

GEORGE: Maybe I will have a little drink.

(As DEE prepares GEORGE's drink:)

DEE: He comes equipped with his own key light.

GEORGE: Hey, I like that one.

DEE: He never met a mirror he didn't like.

(Pause)

DEE & GEORGE: But with good reason.

(Music up: a song like "Holla Back Girl" as bar slides in. CHI CHI sitting at bar, nursing a drink. An exhausted

ANGEL *enters, sees him, makes a face of distaste and turns to leave.)*

CHI CHI: Oh, sit jour ass down, hootchie mama. I don't bite.

(ANGEL sits.)

ANGEL: Eyes in the back of your head?

CHI CHI: Or a mirrored back splash on the bar, take jour pick.

ANGEL: Oh. *(He immediately checks himself in the mirror.)* So can a role model have a drink?

CHI CHI: Are ju finished for today?

ANGEL: Yes, warden.

CHI CHI: *(To* BARTENDER*)* Champagne. Make it good.

(ANGEL smiles, sits.)

ANGEL: You remembered.

CHI CHI: Lucky guess, that's all.

ANGEL: Uh huh. When George and I are finally married I'm redecorating and the first thing that's going is you. I'm supposed to meet him here, where is he?

CHI CHI: Maybe he finally woke up from the nightmare that is Angel and is moving heaven and hell to be as far away from ju as humanly possible.

ANGEL: ...So, you're saying he's stuck in traffic?

CHI CHI: Jeah, probably. So, ju have fun today?

(ANGEL gives CHI CHI the death stare. CHI CHI stifles a laugh.)

CHI CHI: Sorry.

ANGEL: I never knew the needy could be so, ...needy.

CHI CHI: Jeah, how about that?

ANGEL: It's always about them. Me me me me me. I just don't understand people like that.

CHI CHI: Well how could ju.

(BARTENDER *gives* ANGEL *his drinks,* ANGEL *drains it in one gulp and motions for another.*)

ANGEL: I'm supposed to keep a smile on my face for the photographers while I'm changing some baby's dirty diaper.

(CHI CHI *blurts out a laugh, stops himself.*)

CHI CHI: I'm sorry, I just got a mental image of that.

ANGEL: You're really enjoying this, aren't you?

(CHI CHI *shrugs.*)

ANGEL: Well, you can send me out everyday from dawn to dusk and I'll keep going because I have my eye on the prize. My name is going to be Angel Lanier, I will be married to George and there's nothing you can do to stop it.

CHI CHI: No, there isn't; but I can make you a little more worthy.

ANGEL: Now, Chi Chi, dear, you must know once I'm married I'll never go back to those hell holes. Ever.

CHI CHI: But by then they'll get some more publicity, their donations will go up and maybe they can help some more people. It's all about awareness, Angel.

ANGEL: More like torture.

CHI CHI: C'mon, it wasn't that bad, was it?

(ANGEL *downs another champagne.*)

CHI CHI: Guess it was.

(BARTENDER *refills* ANGEL's *glass.*)

CHI CHI: Just a total waste, huh?

ANGEL: Total. *(Silence)* Okay, I go to this, like AIDS testing place with all the press. Mind you I have not had a thing to eat all day. So I'm there and this woman is called to get her medication or whatever and she has a baby and she gives it to me. To me! I'm like, what do I do with this?! This kid is like two years old, takes one look at me and slugs me. Right in the nose. All the eyes of the press are on me so I just keep smiling at this little creature and he starts crying; and I think to myself, "I got nothing". Crying babies, me, not a good mix. I'm panic stricken, my eyebrows shoot up to the top of my head and he stops crying. Just like that. So I start wiggling my eyebrows at him and he starts to laugh. Really. Deeply. Laugh. When his mother came back I handed him off to her and as I got on the elevator I see this little kid using his hands to raise his eyebrows up and down. ...Okay, that part of the day was not a total waste of time.

CHI CHI: Why *puta* boy, did ju just have jourself a little moment?

ANGEL: Certainly not. *(Is about to drain his drink, stops.)* And please, don't call me that again.

CHI CHI: Okay, how about pushy bottom?

ANGEL: You know, if I've learned anything in life is when a gay man can't have you he automatically calls you a bottom. Nice way of saving face.

(This time CHI CHI drinks, avoiding eye contact.)

ANGEL: Not as dumb as I look, am I? Do I make you nervous, Chi Chi?

CHI CHI: *(Loudly)* I need a drink here!

ANGEL: You know what I think, Chi Chi?

CHI CHI: Oh God.

ANGEL: I think you think about me day and night. I think when you saw me naked in George's office it became the screen saver to your soul and in spite of everything you say about me I think you'd do anything for one night with me.

(CHI CHI *studies* ANGEL. BARTENDER *refills* CHI CHI's *drink, smiles at* CHI CHI *who doesn't notice, but* ANGEL *does.*)

CHI CHI: Please tell me I would be armed during this night.

ANGEL: Well, I've never needed accessories, but if it makes it more interesting for you, sure. Why are you alone, Chi Chi? You're not a bad looking guy.

(*Off* CHI CHI's *doubtful look:*)

ANGEL: I mean it. Look, I'll raise my hand when I'm telling the truth. (*He raises his hand.*) You're kind of good looking, in a second string kind of way.

CHI CHI: Wow, that means so much to me coming from ju.

ANGEL: Raise your hand so I'll know you're telling the truth.

(CHI CHI *takes a sip from his drink instead.*)

ANGEL: Tell me, do I keep you up at night?

(CHI CHI *takes* ANGEL *in.*)

CHI CHI: Okay, …I'll give it to ju. I think jou're very good looking.

(*He raises his hand.*)

ANGEL: Now that wasn't so bad, was it?

CHI CHI: In fact, jou're beautiful.

(CHI CHI *raises his hand again.* ANGEL *smiles.*)

CHI CHI: Like a beautifully decorated cake with nothing inside.

(ANGEL's *smile fades.*)

ANGEL: And yet, every man in this bar wants this particular cake. And so do you.

CHI CHI: Nah, junk food gives me cavities.

ANGEL: You don't want me?

CHI CHI: No, I don't.

ANGEL: You didn't raise your hand.

(CHI CHI *raises his hand.*)

ANGEL: Maybe I should have made this simpler for you. You raise your hand when you're telling the truth, not when you're lying.

CHI CHI: I've had beautiful men, ju know, I've had really gorgeous sexy men. I've slept with so many men I can't even remember them all. It never made me feel any better. It was supposed to, but it didn't.

ANGEL: You must have been doing it wrong, that's all.

CHI CHI: Oh baby, no, I can make bedroom walls sweat. The pretty boys like ju.

ANGEL: You said beautiful, remember?

CHI CHI: Their eyes roll back in their heads and they start speaking in tongues. It must be a religious experience because they keep saying, "Oh God, oh God, oh God." (*Silence*) Do I make ju nervous?

(*Silence*)

ANGEL: Didn't you love that they all thought you were special?

CHI CHI: No, cause I didn't think I was special.

ANGEL: So, what, now you don't have sex?

CHI CHI: Unless I can talk to them in the morning I don't want to have sex with them the night before.

ANGEL: And how's that working out for you?

CHI CHI: I haven't had sex in a year and a half.

ANGEL: ...Raise your hand and say that.

(CHI CHI does.)

CHI CHI: Eighteen months. No sex.

ANGEL: Are you telling me, that on the off chance, the very off chance, I would say yes to you you'd say—

CHI CHI: No. Because I want more.

(He raises his hand. Suggested music: a few bars of "Isn't It Romantic." We go to DEE and GEORGE who are slow dancing. badly. Very badly. GEORGE has taken off his jacket. They are both happy drunk.)

DEE: I think we may be the only two gay men in the whole wide world who can't dance. I mean, if you can't dance to Sinatra you might as well give up.

GEORGE: I never know who's supposed to lead.

DEE: Always a problem. Okay, show me what you've got, big guy.

(DEE steps back as GEORGE continues dancing as if he were holding someone, his arms outstreched before him. He is very stiff.)

DEE: Just concentrate on going side to side.

GEORGE: How am I doing?

DEE: I'm going to try to get in there.

GEORGE: You're a braver man than I am.

(DEE takes another sip from his drink. he begins swaying side to side, trying to time his movements with GEORGE. It is not pretty.)

DEE: It's like double dutch. It's all about the timing.

(DEE *and* GEORGE *miss.*)

GEORGE: That wasn't bad, that was kind of close.

DEE: Close won't cut it with Angel. Let's try this again.

GEORGE: I better sit this one out. You go on ahead without me.

DEE: Don't mind if I do. (*He begins to dance by himself.*)

GEORGE: After those two drinks my head is kind of… actually, it feels nice. What were those lethal things?

DEE: White wine spritzers.

GEORGE: I should write that down.

DEE: Listen, when you're dancing with Angel, just follow his lead and you'll be fine.

GEORGE: Yeah, he always knows what to do. Hey, there's another one for the toast. (*His head begins to bob.*) Angel always does the right thing.

(DEE *stops dancing.*)

GEORGE: I hope I don't make him look silly.

DEE: Nothing makes Angel look silly. It's physically impossible.

GEORGE: Hey, you think we can have a conga line at the wedding? Or is that too…

DEE: You can have whatever you want.

GEORGE: Chi Chi would like the conga line. I love my Chi Chi. I love my Dee, too.

DEE: You're just full of love tonight, aren't you. We need to pour you into a cab.

GEORGE: My car's waiting downstairs.

DEE: Ah yes, the lifestyles of the rich and famous.

GEORGE: More like infamous. I love my Angel but
I miss him. It's never just us two anymore. We've
become an event.

DEE: It'll die down, you'll see.

GEORGE: No it won't. Angel won't let it. He loves the
attention. Told me just the other day, right up front
about it. ...Hey, there's something else for the toast, do
you know my Angel has never lied to me. Ever.

DEE: How about that.

(GEORGE *is having trouble putting on his jacket.*)

GEORGE: I'm a very lucky man. And so is your Danny.

(DEE *helps* GEORGE *with his jacket.*)

DEE: Here, you've got that jacket all twisted up.

(DEE *is helping* GEORGE *with the jacket. They are facing
each other again. slowly,* GEORGE *begins to sway back and
forth and before they know it they are dancing again, not
really sure how it happened.*)

GEORGE: This is nice.

(*The music stops,* DEE *and* GEORGE *continue dancing in
silence.* GEORGE *begins to hum the song they were just
dancing to. They continue dancing.*)

DEE: It's getting late.

(GEORGE *looks at his watch.*)

GEORGE: I'll say, I was supposed to meet Angel an hour
ago.

(DEE *panics.*)

DEE: What?! Oh my God! Oh no! This is terrible! Okay,
uh, quick, your car, got stalled, no stolen!, that's better,
and your phone, it was in the car! And just apologize
all over the place. Keep saying how sorry you are.

GEORGE: I forgot, that's all.

DEE: Please, promise me whatever you say, promise me you won't say that! Anything but that! You can never forget Angel. Go, go, go, go, go!

GEORGE: Okay, I'm going, I'm going. *(At the door)* I had a great time.

DEE: I did too, goodbye.

GEORGE: But we're not done, with the toast. So, I'll be back. If that's okay.

DEE: Of course, you're Angel's fiancee.

GEORGE: And your friend, hopefully . I can't believe I'm leaving and I still haven't replaced your ring.

DEE: Danny will get me another one. Goodbye.

GEORGE: I'm sure he will. You're a keeper. You're the kind of guy somebody could build a forever with. Good night. *(He leaves.)*

DEE: Good night, George. *(He picks up Danny's picture. To Danny's smiling image:)* Oh, shut up.

(We go back to ANGEL *and* CHI CHI *sitting at the bar.)*

ANGEL: We both want more. The only difference is I'll get mine. You? I'm not too sure about.

CHI CHI: Jou're worried about me. That's so sweet. Either that or jou're drunk.

ANGEL: Could be both. Hey! After I marry George I'll be kind of like your boss.

CHI CHI: Okay, I'm cutting ju off.

*(*ANGEL *takes* CHI CHI*'s drink.)*

ANGEL: Now tell the truth, if there were no George, you'd make a play for me, wouldn't you?

CHI CHI: Play time's over. Gimme back my drink.

*(*ANGEL *takes a sip of the drink.)*

ANGEL: A little strong but I could get used to the taste.

(CHI CHI takes back his drink.)

ANGEL: And I bet you could, too.

CHI CHI: Cut it out.

ANGEL: Hey, Mr Lopez, am I your Achilles' heel? *(He begins to playfully tap CHI CHI on the shoulder.)* Hey, Chi Chi, I'm talking to you.

(In a rage, CHI CHI turns to face him, spilling his drink. Awkward silence as ANGEL quickly sobers up and BARTENDER wipes up the spilt drink.)

ANGEL: I was just playing is all.

CHI CHI: Are ju playing with George?

ANGEL: ...I play with everybody. It's just who I am.

(CHI CHI throws some money on the bar and gets up to leave.)

ANGEL: Wait, come on, you're causing a scene. Don't go. Look, I'll buy you a drink. I never buy anybody a drink.

CHI CHI: I'm a little particular about who I let buy me a drink.

ANGEL: Please. Stay. I hate being alone in a bar. I really do.

(CHI CHI pats ANGEL's shoulder and points to the mirror in front of them.)

CHI CHI: As long as ju got a mirror in front of ju jou'll never be alone.

(GEORGE enters.)

GEORGE: Sorry I'm late.

(ANGEL Immeditaley hugs and kisses GEORGE.)

ANGEL: Oh George. *(Lots of little kisses all over GEORGE's face.)* Thank goodness you're here. Chi Chi is being a total bore and, ...Have you been drinking?

GEORGE: Sshh. No questions allowed. Dee and me are planning a little surprise for my Angel.

CHI CHI: Sounds like fun.

ANGEL: I hate surprises unless I know about them in advance.

GEORGE: *(To* BARTENDER*)* White wine spritzer, please.

*(*GEORGE *begins to hum,* Isn't It Romantic. ANGEL *and* CHI CHI *stare at him.)*

ANGEL: George. You're humming.

GEORGE: Oh. Am I? Sorry.

*(*GEORGE *smiles and continues humming. He looks over to* DEE*'s area and* CHI CHI *follows* GEORGE*'s stare towards* DEE. *Lights out on* DEE. GRETCHEN *enters, still in her wedding dress, now a little worse for wear.* BREE *enters, followed by her date,* TOY.*)*

BREE: There you are. Tout of society is here.

GRETCHEN: Oh and us.

BREE: All right, so we're relegated to Siberia, but at least we're here.

GRETCHEN: Do you think our unfortunate seating assignments have anything to do with my attire?

BREE: Well, it is getting a little, uh not so fresh shall we say, but nothing a little Shalimar wouldn't fix. *(She takes out a little bottle and sprays* GRETCHEN *with it.)* There, almost tolerable.

GRETCHEN: What a unique flavor sensation. Broken vows and overpriced perfume. By the by, who's the…?

BREE: Stiff? I just call him Toy. He's brand new and I just had to show him off. Oh, and look.

*(*BREE *presses her palms together and* TOY *twitches.)*

GRETCHEN: Good lord!

BREE: Chastity belt. Remote controlled. *(Shows her right palm.)* I just send a volt jolt to his nether regions every time he needs to be reminded he only has eyes for me.

GRETCHEN: Well, you've finally lost it. What little you had.

BREE: Jealous?

GRETCHEN: Certainly not.

BREE: I know where my Toy is morning, noon and night which is more than I could have said for either of our husbands.

GRETCHEN: And he...?

BREE: Loves it! To a degree of course. It has made for some interesting contre temps at metal detectors, but I figure our name is mud anyway so might as well just go for the gusto.

GRETCHEN: You really think we should?

BREE: My dear, who's to stop us?

GRETCHEN: Are you saying that we should follow our heart, no matter what anyone else says? That it's not for other people to judge us and our love but for us to bravely stand by who and what makes us happy?

BREE: No, I just like to see this guy jump around is all.

(GRETCHEN suddenly embraces BREE.)

GRETCHEN: Oh Bree!

BREE: Easy, you're still a little ripe.

GRETCHEN: I'm taking Seth back!

BREE: Back where? He's in the big house.

GRETCHEN: I've tried to follow your lead, to stop loving him, but I can't.

BREE: Try harder. Here, jolt the boy. It's fabulous! Press the little button.

(BREE *presses the remote into* GRETCHEN'*s unwilling hand.*)

BREE: Years of resentment just roll right off you.

GRETCHEN: It's easier for you, you never loved Fletcher.

BREE: Well, of course not, I was married to the man.

(BREE *takes the remote from* GRETCHEN *and presses the button, long and hard.* TOY *has a spasm.*)

BREE: Oh, that was a good one!!

GRETCHEN: But Seth loved me. I know he did. He's the man I love and I want to grow old with him.

BREE: I'm not hearing this.

(BREE *presses her hands against her ears, which of course presses the button on the remote causing* TOY *to spasm as he falls to the floor. She tries to drown out* GRETCHEN.)

BREE: La, la, la, la, la!!

(GRETCHEN *grabs* BREE'*s hands away from her ears, releasing the pressure on the remote.* TOY *is able to catch his breath and stand.*)

GRETCHEN: Bree, I cannot stop loving him because people want me to.

BREE: What about if he wants you to? All your little visits to him in the slammer, I know about them, do you think he'd be so happy to see you if you weren't bringing him gifts?!

GRETCHEN: Yes, maybe, I…don't know.

BREE: Maybe you should find out.

GRETCHEN: Maybe I should. Oh Bree!

BREE: Oh Gretchen!

(BREE *and* GRETCHEN *hug, pressing once again the button on the remote. The ladies hug is actually quite heartfelt, which of course means the pressure on the button is too.* TOY *is rolling around on the ground.*)

BREE: Run! Run like the wind, you fairy princess you!!

(A happy GRETCHEN *runs off.)*

BREE: Emphasis on the fairy.

*(*BREE *looks down to where* TOY *is panting, trying to catch his breath.)*

BREE: Oh, sorry about that.

TOY: ...Do you...do you think that maybe we could up the voltage on that thing?

(Big smile from BREE. *Music: a song like "Stepping Out."*
Four doors open in the back, we see the silhouettes of four
men, lights up to reveal the tuxedoed men as they enter.
GEORGE, DEE, CHI CHI *and* ANGEL. CHI CHI *and* GEORGE
go to one side while ANGEL *and* DEE *go to the other side.*
In silhouette we see a PHOTOGRAPHER *and a* REPORTER
documenting ANGEL*'s happy day as* ANGEL *does his final*
preparation with DEE, *his heart broken,* ATTENDANT. *On*
the other side we see the silhouette of GEORGE, *nervously*
pacing as CHI CHI *is trying to tie his tie. Lights up to full on*
CHI CHI *and* GEORGE, *who is still working on memorizing*
his toast to ANGEL.)

GEORGE: ...and then I say, thank you to all our honored guests, but the most important person here is—

CHI CHI: Anybody but Angel.

GEORGE: Anybody but Angel—stop that! I'm already nervous enough as it is.

CHI CHI: Lissen baby, I got a full tank of gas and the motor running, we could be in Miami beach by daybreak.

GEORGE: Why are you the best man again?

CHI CHI: Because I'm always the best man.

*(*DEE *enters.)*

DEE: I just wanted to wish you well and— Wow. You look…great.

GEORGE: …Yeah, you too.

(Silence)

CHI CHI: Well, ju two are some snappy conversationalists I gotta tell ju. Dee, would ju help him with this thing. I gotta check on something I'm so sure. *(He exits.)*

DEE: Nervous.

GEORGE: Panic stricken.

DEE: Don't be.

GEORGE: I always dreamed of getting married, just never thought I would.

DEE: Never thought you'd fall in love?

GEORGE: …Maybe we should practice the dance one more time.

DEE: No. You're fine. You're more than fine. You're perfect. Which is why you and Angel belong together. Because you're both perfect. You got your toast written down?

GEORGE: *(Points to breast pocket)* In here.

DEE: Don't be embarrassed to look at it if you need to.

*(*GEORGE's *hand is still over his heart.)*

DEE: And if you get lost you can always just speak from the heart.

GEORGE: All of a sudden I've forgotten everything. I don't know what I would say, except that I love you— *(Corrects himself)* —him, and that ever since we met my life has changed and I can't imagine my life without him— *(Corrects himself)* —you. Without you. Dee…. Can I kiss you?

DEE: No.

(GEORGE kisses DEE, who holds for a moment then breaks free.)

GEORGE: You were the person I didn't know I was looking for, hidden away in plain view and I don't want anything except to wake up everyday for the rest of my life next to you.

(GEORGE tries to kiss DEE again, but DEE holds him back.)

DEE: *(Shaking his head, pointing to parts of himself)* No, no, you want Angel, not me. Look at me. I mean, really look at me. These are love handles, and this is a bald spot that is not going to get any smaller and this is the beginning of a double chin. I'm the best friend. That's who I'm supposed to be, that's all I am—

(GEORGE grabs DEE and really kisses him. DEE loses himself in the kiss. CHI CHI reenters, sees their kiss.)

CHI CHI: *(To himself)* Finally.

(Lights out on them and up on ANGEL and the press.)

REPORTER: Where will you two honeymoon?

ANGEL: If I told you that the press would be all over us. But if you do happen to catch a glimpse of my travel itinerary on the table, well that certainly wouldn't be my fault.

(PHOTOGRAPHER takes a picture of the itinerary as CHI CHI enters.)

CHI CHI: I'm sorry but ju gentlemen are going to have to take jour seats for the show now.

ANGEL: You mean the wedding.

CHI CHI: Isn't that what I said?

(The press leaves, CHI CHI sits and smiles.)

ANGEL: The wedding's out there, you may want to join them.

CHI CHI: Oh I think the fun is gonna be in here.

(Go back to GEORGE *and* DEE.*)*

GEORGE: I'm so sorry, I have no right to say anything to you, much less that I love you.

DEE: No, you love Angel.

GEORGE: And you love Danny. But I can't help it, I love you.

DEE: You love me?

*(*GEORGE *nods.)*

DEE: Are you bobbing or nodding?

GEORGE: I love you.

DEE: Hold that thought. *(He runs out and into* ANGEL's *area.)*

CHI CHI: What kept ju? Ju take the local?

ANGEL: Dee, finally. Chi Chi's been undressing me with his eyes and, well, I didn't think it was appropriate on my wedding day.

DEE: Angel, I'm sorry, …you can't, you can't…

ANGEL: Let's see, I'm sure I've got everything. Something old, something new, something borrowed, something blue.

CHI CHI: Something stolen.

ANGEL: Are you still here?

DEE: I'm sorry, but you can't…

CHI CHI: Spit it out!

DEE: You can't marry George. You can't.

ANGEL: *(Tenderly)* Oh Dee.

DEE: You…can't because…

(Music starts underneath.)

ANGEL: That music tells me otherwise.

DEE: Please, he...

ANGEL: Isn't you. I know. Why couldn't you have been born rich instead of loyal?

CHI CHI: *(To DEE)* For once in jour life, stand up for jourself.

ANGEL: *(To CHI CHI)* You can wait outside.

CHI CHI: Dee, if ju love him, you have to fight for him.

ANGEL: Goodbye Chi Chi.

DEE: You can't marry George, ...because I love him.

(ANGEL stops.)

DEE: I love him. Oh my God, I do. I really do. I'm sorry.

ANGEL: Well, seeing as I'm about to marry the man, this is very inconvenient.

CHI CHI: Keep going.

DEE: And he loves me, too.

ANGEL: No. George loves me. *(Silence)* Say it. Say, "George loves you, Angel". Say it. Dee. Please.

(Silence)

DEE: I can't.

ANGEL: Well. That's too bad. You can't have him.

DEE: Angel—

ANGEL: I said no! How could you?!

DEE: I didn't mean for this to happen.

ANGEL: You have somebody. How would you like it if I stole Danny away from you?

CHI CHI: Let's ask him, here's Danny now. *(He steps aside, opens a door, there is no one there.)*

DEE: You knew?

ANGEL: Knew what? Chi Chi, you're an idiot, there's nobody

(*Finally dawns on* ANGEL.)

ANGEL: ...there. There's nobody there. There is no Danny, is there? There never was.

DEE: No.

CHI CHI: Did ju really think Dee would give away the ring of the man he loves? Even for ju?

ANGEL: You lied to me, Dee.

DEE: I'm so sorry.

ANGEL: Why would you lie to me? Why would you make me believe you had a lover?

DEE: Because I wanted you to think somebody wanted me, that I mattered to somebody and that somebody loved me. And then maybe you and everybody else wouldn't think I was so pathetic.

ANGEL: I never thought you were pathetic. I thought you were my friend.

DEE: I am.

ANGEL: No you're not.

DEE: Angel...

ANGEL: You're the only one who could ever break my heart, Dee, because I really loved you.

(GEORGE *enters.*)

CHI CHI: Oh good, the fourth for bridge.

GEORGE: I'm telling them to hold the music.

DEE: No, don't do that.

GEORGE: Yes, but—

DEE: No, it's, it's no use holding up the ceremony. Danny's just not going to make it. And I don't want to ruin my Angel's day.

GEORGE: I think I should talk to Danny.

CHI CHI: There's an idea, let's all talk to Danny.

DEE: No. There's nothing to talk about.

GEORGE: But, Dee—

DEE: No. Now, George, doesn't Angel look perfect?

GEORGE: ...Yes.

DEE: Danny had such a crush on him. Well, everybody did, and does. I hope you know how lucky you are, George.

(ANGEL *takes* GEORGE's *hand.*)

ANGEL: You do, don't you?

GEORGE: I do.

(ANGEL *becomes* ANGEL *again.*)

ANGEL: You just keep saying that. Say you love me.

GEORGE: I love...doing things for you, Angel. I love how your face lights up whenever I give you something, I love...

ANGEL: Don't strain yourself, that's more than enough.

(GEORGE's *head begins to bob.* ANGEL *gently stops it with his hands.*)

ANGEL: I thought we had that under control. Don't you worry. We will.

DEE: I'm going to take my place.

GEORGE: You're not walking Angel down the aisle?

DEE: No, this is his moment. (*To* ANGEL) You look...

ANGEL: I know.

(ANGEL *hugs* DEE.)

DEE: That music isn't on a loop, you two better get out there. *(He exits.)*

GEORGE: Chi Chi, can I have a minute with Angel?

ANGEL: No. Stay Chi Chi. *(He makes a face of distaste.)* Didn't think I'd ever say that.

ANGEL: *(To* GEORGE*)* You're going to have me for an entire lifetime after the wedding. Now, you get out there and wait for me. Go on.

*(*GEORGE *starts out.)*

ANGEL: Hey George. We're going to get married, and everybody who said that we couldn't is out there. We'll show them. Won't they be surprised.

*(*GEORGE *exits.)*

CHI CHI: Ju know.

ANGEL: Don't. *(He checks himself in the mirror, he takes a flute of champagne and downs it.)*

(Off ANGEL*'s looking at himself.)*

CHI CHI: I'm surprised you can still look at yourself.

ANGEL: Why not? I'm about to marry the richest man in the world.

*(*ANGEL *walks out, all eyes are on him. Followed by* CHI CHI *who falls in step alongside him, refusing to give up.* GEORGE *waits at the other end as* ANGEL *and* CHI CHI *walk towards him.)*

ANGEL: *(Hisses)* What the hell are you doing? Get away from me!

CHI CHI: Ju gotta look at that little piece of real estate ju call a heart and do the right thing, for once in jour selfish life.

ANGEL: I'm the one who was lied to! I'm the injured party, Spanish Fly.

CHI CHI: Dee has done nothing but love ju his entire life.

ANGEL: Oh, you mean when he wasn't stealing George away from me? George belongs to me, period. He's mine, I love him and I'm marrying him.

CHI CHI: No, Dee loves him.

ANGEL: He'll get over it.

CHI CHI: No he won't. Dee would love George even if he didn't have a dime to his name. And as much as he loves George he loves ju, too. Why am I even wasting my breath with ju. Because I think that somewhere inside ju is a man who could love somebody more than he loves himself. Tell me I'm not wrong.

ANGEL: Dee will be okay, I'll always take care of him.

CHI CHI: And will ju find him somebody else who loves him the way George does? Can ju do that?

(They have reached the justice of the peace. GEORGE is standing there waiting for ANGEL. CHI CHI makes one last ditch effort.)

CHI CHI: Fine. You take Dee's ring and marry the man he loves. Break his heart. I dare ju. Forget everything he's ever done for ju. All the times he put ju first. I never thought ju loved George, but I thought ju loved Dee.

JUSTICE OF THE PEACE: *(To* CHI CHI*)* Excuse me, young man, I've got it from here. *(To* GEORGE*)* George Lanier, do you take Angel as your husband, from this day forward, in sickness and in health for richer or poorer, as long as you both shall live?

GEORGE: I...do.

JUSTICE OF THE PEACE: Yes, and do you Angel take George Lanier as your husband from this day forward, in sickness and in health, for richer or poorer, as long as you both shall live? *(Silence)* …Young man?

CHI CHI: *(Under his breath)* C'mon Angel. C'mon.

ANGEL: What?

JUSTICE OF THE PEACE: It's your turn now. *(Silence)* Do you take George Lanier—

ANGEL: Yes. I mean, …I…I…can't. I'm sorry, George. I am so sorry. Really. You have no idea how sorry I am, but I can't, …because, well, because…I'm in love with Danny. Yes. That's it. I'm sorry, Dee, but Danny and I have been having an affair, forever almost, I don't even know when it started, but we're in love.

DEE: Angel.

CHI CHI: Sssh. Angel's got the floor now.

ANGEL: Danny is someone who has given up so much for me. Even when all I did was take. And I can finally show him how much he means to me. Because he does. And he has the most beautiful smile in the world. Even with that little gap in his teeth. So, I can't marry you George. I realize that now. I'm sorry. And Dee, please forgive me, but Danny and I love each other, like you and George do, so you see, this is your place up here. Next to George. Because people who love each other belong together. Even I know that. Or maybe I've finally learned that. I belong with Danny and you belong here, with George.

(ANGEL holds out his hand to DEE who rises. ANGEL takes off the gold band, hands it to DEE. He kisses DEE on the nose.)

ANGEL: This is yours. *(Points to GEORGE)* And so is he.

(DEE takes his rightful place by GEORGE, they kiss. JUSTICE OF THE PEACE clears his throat.)

JUSTICE OF THE PEACE: We're still short an "I do".

DEE: I do.

GEORGE: Boy, do I.

JUSTICE OF THE PEACE: By the power vested in me I now declare you husband and husband.

(DEE and GEORGE kiss again. DEE breaks the kiss to look at ANGEL, who points him forward.)

ANGEL: Go.

(DEE and GEORGE exit, with guests following throwing rice. BREE continously jolts TOY, causing him to miss. ANGEL and CHI CHI are now alone. Silence)

CHI CHI: An angel earns his wings.

ANGEL: Embrace the cliche why don't you.

DEE: So, …ju want to go get drunk?

ANGEL: God yes!!

CHI CHI: Ju know, right at this moment, I'm beginning to like ju and that scares me.

ANGEL: It won't do wonders for my beauty sleep either, trust me.

(ANGEL and CHI CHI share an awkward laugh. Silence. Then suddenly kiss passionately. They break apart, study each other. Zip)

CHI CHI: Nothing.

ANGEL: You're telling me.

(Pause. Or maybe not "zip". As ANGEL and CHI CHI walk off.)

CHI CHI: Two out of three?

ANGEL: You wish.

CHI CHI: No, baby, ju wish.

END OF PLAY